READING AND WRITING STRATEGICALLY

RAISING THE BAR OF EXPECTATIONS

Second Edition

Wendell Christensen and Lianne Fernández

www.readingandwritingstrategically.com

PREFACE

In order to fully comprehend reading, and be an effective writer, the learner is expected to internalize a multitude of strategies. It is our hope that you will use *Reading and Writing Strategically* like an archer uses arrows from a quiver. When one strategy is ineffective for a student, reach into the book for another strategy, like the archer does when the target is missed. Our aim is for you to realize that literacy is an interwoven process, much like that of a braid of rope, all pieces needing each other in order to form a whole product.

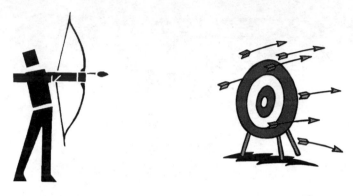

Today's methodologies contradict the "old school" method of teaching where the teacher simply followed a basal. Students do not learn by turning from one page to the next in predetermined steps or sequences, at prescribed times. In order for students to acquire knowledge, teaching **must** be recursive. It is much like the pendulum that slowly sweeps backward before moving forward.

Before you begin your journey through *Reading & Writing Strategically*, keep in mind that, the two most important factors that will determine your students' success in the classroom are: **"the delivery of your instruction"** and having **"withitness."** If after perusing through our book, you would like more information and examples, or even have some comments, please contact us at www.readingandwritingstrategically.com. We will kindly respond to your questions and comments through e-mails. **ENJOY!**

TABLE OF CONTENTS

SECTION 1: HOW TO REACH STUDENTS

SECTION 2: LANGUAGE DEVELOPMENT AND ACTIVITIES

SECTION 3: READING COMPREHENSION STRATEGIES AND ACTIVITIES

SECTION 4: WRITING STRATEGIES AND ACTIVITIES

SECTION 5: GRAPHIC ORGANIZERS

SECTION 6: REFLECTIONS AND REFERENCES

Throughout the table of contents, we have correlated our strategies and activities to the NCTE standards. With this in mind, we have chosen those standards that are closely aligned, and noted them in parenthesis. Additionally, please be aware that all of the standards are interrelated and should be considered as a whole. A special note: The Graphic Organizer section lists all of the standards under one section, however, depending upon how each is used, they can be identified in one standard or another.

**CHALLENGING STUDENTS TO
WORK SMARTER**

USING MULTIPLE STRATEGIES

SECTION 1
HOW TO REACH STUDENTS

EFFECTIVE MODELING

DELIVERY OF INSTRUCTION

REFLECTIVE PRACTICE

OVERVIEW

Research indicates there is a strong relationship between reading and effective writing. Studies show that an active reader, one who analyzes passages and makes logical predictions before and during reading, uses higher-order thinking skills associated with effective writing. Active readers prepare for reading by using illustrations, titles, and sub-heading cues and by analyzing passages through self-questioning, predicting, skimming, and summarizing.

EFFECTIVE READERS:

❖ Want to keep reading on their own.

❖ Use prior knowledge to understand the author's purpose.

❖ Infer, predict, confirm, and incorporate reading into their bank of knowledge.

❖ Self-evaluate, reflect, and question before, during, and after reading.

EFFECTIVE WRITERS:

❖ Incorporate elements in such a way that a reader can experience the writer's intended meaning, understand the writer's premise, and accept or reject the writer's point of view.

❖ Focus on the topic and avoid extraneous or loosely related information.

❖ Establish a clear organizational pattern (beginning, middle, and end with meaningful transitional devices).

❖ Contain supporting ideas that are elaborated through the use of details, examples, vivid language, and mature word choice.

❖ Follow the conventions of standard written English (punctuation, capitalization, and spelling) and include a variety of sentence structures.

Laura Robb (1996) defines "*skills* as a set of helpful tools that students practice in order to improve reading. A skill becomes a *strategy* when the learner can use it independently, when he/she can reflect on and understand how it works and then apply it to new material." It is our hope that you teach your students the *skills* they need to turn in to *strategies* for lifelong educational success.

It is intended that you use the strategies and activities included within as a framework to prepare students for writing and better reading comprehension. Many of the materials have been adapted from teaching professionals, personal experiences, and of course, reflections, and feedback from those whom we teach, our students.

WHY STRATEGIES?

Why is teaching strategies so important? Within one classroom setting, there are a wide variety of different learning styles. One single method taught one way would not reach all of your students. Traditional methods of instruction are no longer sufficient to meet the needs of today's students. The more we get to know how students learn, the more we must adjust our methods of teaching. Learning is an active, social process. As teachers, we need to talk less and listen more!

Teaching strategies empowers students with the tools they need in order to be successful readers and writers. Learning becomes their responsibility. As they navigate through a modeled lesson, students choose which strategy will help them connect with the task and be able to experiment and try their newly acquired knowledge. The result? We now have students with the confidence and ability to be independent learners.

We realize that there is no certain or set time when we leave one strategy and introduce another. We do have some practical guidelines that you may wish to follow. To help students get a handle on a strategy, the strategy must be practiced over time from explicit instruction, and guided practice, to assessing the strategy being used by the student.

To assess the strategy in use, travel around the classroom monitoring students. A new strategy should be introduced when we observe our learners applying the strategy across the curriculum in different situations, when it is being overused, or when boredom has set in.

As we work with preschool and kindergarten students, even though we recognize that they may not be able to read or write, remember that teaching strategies is mostly about getting students to think. At this young age, they can give us oral responses; hence, we are teaching students of all ages to learn strategically. As teachers of primary grades, intermediate grades, middle school, and high school receive these students into their classrooms, we begin to understand how important vertical teaching is becoming. It would be ideal if we could build upon strategies, instead of worrying just about content.

We introduce one strategy at a time by modeling it repeatedly. Then, when we feel that the students have "ownership" of the strategy, it is used in one of the classroom centers for constant review and practice.

The following "Another Brick in the Wall" works vertically and horizontally. We have included key strategies and activities. Strategies on the far left are the initial strategies to teach at the beginning of the school year. As you work from left to right, the strategies build upon one another. As you travel vertically, the strategies will become more difficult (varying degrees of sophistication) as students are more familiar with them from year to year. Of course, you would adjust the strategies to meet the needs of the students you are currently working with.

The Strategy Chart is another way to look at the strategies by objective.

ANOTHER BRICK IN THE WALL

H I G H	I DON'T KNOW… TRAFFIC COURT	DOODLES-DETAILS WORD MANIA	SENTENCE EXT. GRAPHIC ORG.	SENTENCE COMB.
	MAKING WORDS R, H & S, T & S WORD JAR Q.A.R.	SUMMARIZING N, E, IN THE MARGIN POWER NOTES JUST TWO		HIGHLIGHT THE BEST RECIPROCAL TCH. CLOZE E.I.P.
M I D D L E	I DON'T KNOW… TRAFFIC COURT	DOODLES-DETAILS WORD MANIA	SENTENCE EXT. GRAPHIC ORG.	SENTENCE COMB.
	MAKING WORDS R, H & S, T & S WORD JAR O.A.R.	SUMMARIZING N, E, IN THE MARGIN POWER NOTES JUST TWO		HIGHLIGHT THE BEST RECIPROCAL TCH. CLOZE E.I.P.
5	SENTENCE EXT. WORD MANIA	SENTENCE COMB. I DON'T KNOW… GRAPHIC ORG.	PIGGYBACKING TRAFFIC COURT	SHARING THE PEN DOODLES-DETAILS
	MAKING WORDS R, H & S, T & S WORD WALL WORD JAR	JUST TWO CLOZE Q.A.R. KWL E.I.P.		HIGHLIGHT THE BEST SUMMARIZING N, E RECIPROCAL TCH. IN THE MARGIN POWER NOTES
4	DOODLES-DETAILS I DON'T KNOW…	SENTENCE COMB. SENTENCE EXT.	TRAFFIC COURT SHARING THE PEN	PIGGYBACKING GRAPHIC ORG.
	MAKING WORDS WORD WALL WORD JAR	R, H & S, T & S JUST TWO CLOZE Q.A.R.		HIGHLIGHT THE BEST RECIPROCAL TCH. IN THE MARGIN KWL
3	DOODLES-DETAILS I DON'T KNOW … MAKING WORDS WORD WALL WORD JAR	PIGGYBACKING TRAFFIC COURT R, H & S, T & S WORD MANIA JUST TWO	SENTENCE COMB. SENTENCE EXT. CLOZE Q.A.R. KWL	RECIPROCAL TCH. SHARING THE PEN HIGHLIGHT BEST E.I.P.
2	MAKING WORDS WORD WALL WORD JAR JUST TWO	TRAFFIC COURT R, H & S, T & S WORD MANIA CLOZE		SHARING THE PEN Q.A.R. KWL
1	DOODLES-DETAILS MAKING WORDS WORD WALL	TRAFFIC COURT R, H & S, T & S JUST TWO	WORD MANIA CLOZE	WORD JAR Q.A.R. KWL

STRATEGY CHART

OBJECTIVE	STRATEGY	
PREDICTING **BRAINSTORMING** **& PREVIEWING**	Word Mania	Power Notes
	Doodles-to-Details	SQ3R
	Reciprocal Teaching	KWL
	Sentence Combining	Keys to Voc.
	Guidelines for Asking Questions	Highlight the Best
SELF-QUESTIONING	Traffic Court	R, H&S, T&S
	In the Margin	E.I.P.
	Making Words	SQ3R
	Reciprocal Teaching	Making Conn.
	Guidelines for Asking Questions	Cloze
MONITORING	I Don't Know…	Piggybacking
	Sentence Extension	Keys to Voc.
	R, H&S, T&S	E.I.P.
	Making Connections	Just Two
	Reciprocal Teaching	Making Words
	Guidelines for Asking Questions	Q.A.R.
EVALUATING	I Don't Know…	Piggybacking
	Cloze	KWL
	Sentence Extension	Traffic Court
	Just Two	Making Conn.
	Making Words	Word Walls
	Q.A.R.	SQ3R
SUMMARIZING	Sentence Combining	Summarizing N, E
	In the Margin	Word Mania
	Highlight the Best	SQ3R
	Doodles-to-Details	E.I.P.
	Reciprocal Teaching	Just Two
KEY WORDS & IDEAS	Power Notes	Cloze
	Q.A.R.	E.I.P.
	Doodles-to-Details	Word Mania
	R, H&S, T&S	Making Words
	Highlight the Best	Word Walls
	Vocabulary Mapping	Just Two
	Reciprocal Teaching	

TEACHER'S ROLE

They can do it! When you start out believing this, you begin with the correct mindset to only expect the best! It is not only your job but your obligation to be your best at all times, set high expectations for yourself and for your students, and make sure that you get the most out of your time with your students.

We have no idea what impact we truly have on our students until we hear a colleague repeat something we taught a former student, a parent writes a thank you letter, we receive an invitation to a high school or college graduation or receive a wedding invitation!

Students depend on us to teach them the proper skills and strategies in the most engaging, creative way possible.

How does this all happen?

❖ **Be prepared!** Know what strategy you are concentrating on.
❖ **Preview.** Look over your material ahead of time for possible stopping points, discussion questions, and feedback time.
❖ **Learning style.** Know your students' learning style and be able to reach them at their "Zone of Proximal Development." (See **VYGOTSKY'S THEORY OF LEARNING & GARDNER'S MULTIPLE INTELLIGENCES.**)
❖ **Delivery of instruction.** How you deliver the lesson can make it or break it! Show don't tell!
❖ **Model.** Model what you want the students to learn from the lesson.
❖ **Assess.** Assess the strategy in a variety of ways to allow for individual learning needs.
❖ **Reflective Practice.** Evaluate your own lesson. Did you get the outcome you expected? Are you reaching your students and their learning styles? Changing your practice based upon what worked and what did not work will result in increased academic learning time for your students.

Research overwhelmingly shows that in order for learning to occur, students need to be involved in the process of learning, be provided with hands-on practice, be given multiple chances to show mastery, have time to interact with their peers, be provided with opportunities to work in small groups and given feedback in a timely manner.

Teacher's role?
guide
give guided practice
provide support
model, demonstrate
coach, encourage
interact/be human
repeat all of the above over and over again.

The goal of every teacher should be to assist his or her students with mastery of the "learning how to learn" process. This can be accomplished by gradually releasing the responsibility of learning to the student as new strategies are introduced, therefore producing independent learners. This process is called "scaffolding instruction." With that in mind, how you organize your classroom, and what kind of environment you have, are both important in carrying out your responsibility of ensuring that you have a community of learners that can interact in a safe, caring climate.

Arrangement of your students' desks may vary from teacher to teacher. When you are delivering instruction, desks may be facing you or the speaker so all eyes are on you. Then, there will be times when you want students in cooperative groups.

Materials that are frequently used by students should be in a clear, visible area. Give students a sense of belonging in the classroom by rotating jobs. They can monitor putting away materials, restocking of paper, paper clips, markers, etc.

Student work, not always perfect, should be up and displayed, and changed frequently. When students see that their class work is displayed, they will notice that everything they do has a purpose and is not just busy work. This will also enhance the classroom climate and tell a story about those who work and learn in your classroom.

Consider providing your students a variety of activities that stimulate and engage them in learning to maximize their potential! Remember to provide varying levels of activities to reach all your learners and their learning styles. Give them an environment where they can interact with each other, feel like they are involved and they will take ownership of their own learning. This will result in the goal of making them independent, self-responsible learners.

Let students know that there are many things in the classroom they may have to work on, but there is also a time for flexibility and freedom. The more you make your classroom comfortable, engaging, safe and orderly, the more your students will want to come to school and become active learners.

GARDNER'S MULTIPLE INTELLIGENCES

As you begin to model strategies for your students, it is extremely important to recognize their learning and thinking styles and not just your own. Howard Gardner did just this in his book, *Frames of Mind: The Theory of Multiple Intelligences* in 1983. He has identified seven types of thinking or intelligences. We all possess some part of each one. One or two intelligences are stronger or more developed than the others. By varying the format in which you deliver your instruction and provide for practice with the strategy, you will be reaching far many more students than the traditional method of teaching.

LEARNERS IN THE VERBAL/LINGUISTIC INTELLIGENCE:
(Words and production of language)

- ❖ Enjoy reading, writing, and speaking.
- ❖ Benefit from discussion.
- ❖ Have a good memory for names, places, dates, and details.
- ❖ Like books, records, and tapes.
- ❖ Enjoy storytelling, oral reading, and sharing stories.
- ❖ Enjoy creative writing, poetry, and joke telling. (8)

Strategies for instruction: journal writing, speeches, storytelling, and reading.

LEARNERS IN THE LOGICAL/MATHEMATICAL INTELLIGENCE:
(Numbers, logic, and inductive reasoning)

- ❖ Have good problem solving and reasoning skills.
- ❖ Like to categorize and classify.
- ❖ Like puzzles, mysteries, riddles, and brainteasers.
- ❖ Like technology and computers.
- ❖ Are strong in math. (6)

Strategies for instruction: outlines, codes, calculating, problem solving.

LEARNERS IN THE VISUAL/SPATIAL INTELLIGENCE:
(Pictures, mental images, and sight)

- ❖ Need visuals to understand new concepts.
- ❖ Use mental imagery.
- ❖ Can easily read maps, charts, and diagrams.
- ❖ Enjoy mazes and jigsaw puzzles.
- ❖ Have a strong imagination.
- ❖ Are sensitive to colors.
- ❖ Are good at designing, drawing, creating, and constructing. (11)

Strategies for instruction: drawing, mind-maps, charts.

LEARNERS IN THE BODILY/KINESTHETIC INTELLIGENCE:
(Physical self, control of one's body movements, learns by doing)

* Do well in competitive sports.
* Are well coordinated.
* Like to move around and touch things.
* Use lots of gestures for communicating.
* Like to communicate through drama, dance, and movement.
* Like to spend time outdoors. (13)

Strategies for instruction: role playing, dancing, playing games, and using manipulatives.

LEARNERS IN THE MUSICAL/RHYTHMIC INTELLIGENCE:
(Recognition and use of rhythmic patterns, sensitivity to sounds)

* Enjoy listening and responding to music.
* Know lyrics and melodies.
* Play a musical instrument.
* Are highly aware of sounds in the environment, especially computerized sound systems.
* Learn better while listening to certain types of music. (15)

Strategies for instruction: singing, performing, writing compositions, and choral readings.

LEARNERS IN THE INTERPERSONAL INTELLIGENCE:
(People skills, communication skills, and collaborative skills)

* Have strong leadership and organizational skills.
* Are very sociable and have lots of friends.
* Are good communicators, mediators, and listeners.
* Solve problems by talking through them.
* Learn best by talking to others.
* Enjoy cooperative learning. (19)

Strategies for instruction: working with mentors and tutors, interactive projects, cooperative learning.

LEARNERS IN THE INTRAPERSONAL INTELLIGENCE:
(Inner self, intuition, and emotions)

* Have a sense of independence, self-confidence, and strong will.
* Have good instincts about strengths and abilities.
* Pursue interests, dreams, and goals.
* Like to work independently on projects.
* Like to sit quietly and meditate or reflect. (17)

Strategies for instruction: learning centers, self-reflection tasks, higher-order reasoning.

VYGOTSKY'S THEORY OF LEARNING

Russian psychologist, Lev Vygotsky, believes that learning moves from an initial form of guided learning to later independent learning. He proposed that there are two developmental levels, "actual development" defined as "the level of development of a child's mental functions…determined by independent problem solving." The second, "potential development," and described as "what a person can achieve when given the benefit of support during the task." In other words, it is the ability to solve problems "under adult guidance or in collaboration with more capable peers" (p.86).

Vygotsky identifies the collaborative construction of learning as the Zone of Proximal Development. ZPD (Vygotsky, 1978) is the distance between the actual developmental level of a child and the level of his or her potential development with the guidance of a more capable peer or a teacher.

Vygotsky believes that when a child follows the example of an adult or more capable peer, the child gradually develops the ability to do certain tasks with help or assistance. The outcome is to give the child the independence, confidence, and the security to internalize the task or activity at hand and be able to recall it when necessary.

The Zone of Proximal Development occurs any time in which individuals are in the process of developing knowledge. As teachers, we must provide the level of comfort for students to experiment with new knowledge in a variety of ways, knowing that someone is there for support and encouragement. Once the student continues to exhibit the positive response we are looking for, we gradually start to withdraw our support until the student is performing consistently on his/her own.

The teacher is not the only one that can provide this level of guidance. We always want to be the ones to provide all the instruction and support without realizing that we have students within our own classrooms that can not only assist us but free us up to work with other students. Learning is a social process. The more interaction we provide, the more learning will occur. Students come to us from a multitude of backgrounds and bring to the classroom environment a set of cultures, values, and diverse upbringings. Students interacting with each other and sharing their thoughts and questions, help to build prior knowledge.

It is the ZPD that is critical for learning and instruction. Learning creates the Zone of Proximal Development; it "awakens a variety of internal development processes that are able to operate only when the child is interacting with people in his environment and in cooperation with his peers. Once these processes are internalized, they become part of the child's independent developmental achievement" (p.90).

THE IMPORTANCE OF PRIOR KNOWLEDGE

One of the most universal findings to emerge from recent research is the marked degree in which a learner's prior knowledge of a topic facilitates future comprehension. This prior knowledge or pathway to understanding new ideas, when related to content area assignments is crucial. Content area teachers must take steps to determine students' prior knowledge and background experiences of a topic before deciding if the students can cope with a specific unit of study. (Readence, Bean, & Baldwin, 1985)

❖ Prior knowledge is the totality of what a person knows. It is the organized information inside the head, and roughly synonymous with terms such as *world knowledge, schemata,* and *long-term memory.* (Anthony, Johnson, Mickelson, & Preece, 1991)

❖ Prior knowledge influences strategy use. In some cases, when readers have a great deal of prior knowledge about a domain, they do not use certain strategies because they have less need for them. (Spear-Swerling & Sternberg, 1996)

❖ Comprehension can be thought of as the application of prior knowledge to a current situation. If children are confronted with inauthentic or peculiar language, then their capacity for applying what they know is reduced and their behavior is unlike the behavior they exhibit in normal language use or language-learning situations. (Anthony, Johnson, Mickelson, & Preece, 1991)

❖ Reading comprehension results from the reader's application of prior knowledge to the information made available by the writer in an authored text. Listening comprehension is the application of prior knowledge to oral text such as a speech, lecture reading, or sermon. (Anthony, Johnson, Mickelson, & Preece, 1991)

❖ If everyone's prior knowledge is to some extent unique, then the application of that knowledge to a text will produce an interpretation that is correspondingly unique. (Anthony, Johnson, Mickelson, & Preece, 1991)

In other words, what you already know, determines what you can understand from new passages. Finding out what students know before starting a new topic, not only will guide our instruction but will also activate prior knowledge in others. There are a variety of ways in order to accomplish this. The important thing to remember is that this activating prior knowledge should be oral, engaging, and interacting in order for it to be memorable and meaningful. When students see that their thoughts, ideas and suggestions are validated, they will be more apt to share in other areas of instruction. (See **KWL.**)

FORMULA FOR SUCCESS

It is every teacher's goal to ensure that students can become independent learners within the classroom. In order for this to happen, we must make certain that several key pieces are in place. In isolation, they are quite meaningful, but, when combined in a daily program of instruction and interaction, their importance magnifies.

EXPECTATION Not only should we hold ourselves to high expectations but students also. Regardless of their ability, IQ, background, or walk of life, what you expect is what you get. Just when you think a student cannot do any more, challenge them to try a "little" harder **(Raising the Bar of Expectations)**. Using the right words (verbal) and positive nonverbal behaviors will let the student know that you not only know they can do it, but you EXPECT them to.

MOTIVATION One of the hardest pieces of this formula is motivation. It requires finding what will drive students to try their hardest. Some students may be motivated to work harder if they are sitting near you. Other students may need to work with a peer in order to excel.

ENVIRONMENT This formula will not work if the environment is not conducive to learning. Students must be comfortable with giving an incorrect answer without fear of ridicule. Likewise, if the classroom is set up with engaging walls, meaningful centers, and a cooperative type atmosphere, students will want to try their hardest no matter what the task at hand may be.

DISCOVERY Centers that encourage discovery or a corner with a new unit of study invite students to experiment with new ideas. The classroom should be a place where students are given the opportunity to manipulate activities without always having a clear-cut answer to every problem.

MODELING Without the proper modeling of strategies and skills, students will never be able to become engaged in an activity. It is our job to make sure that we not only model the task at hand repeatedly, but we also model it in a variety of ways. We have many types of learners within the classroom. Teaching a strategy one way will not reach all of our learners. (See **GARDNER'S MULTIPLE INTELLIGENCES.**)

OWNERSHIP Students must feel that what they are learning has some meaning or relevance to them in their life, or it will never become part of their background knowledge. When modeling, or giving an example, connect it to something that is "real" to them. You will then be accomplishing two things: 1) You will have your students' attention; and 2) The new skill or strategy will become part of their memory bank of ideas. They will become responsible for their own learning because they have a vested interest.

PRACTICE Although the other pieces of the formula have their own importance, without meaningful practice, everything is a waste. There is a time and place for so called "ditto" or "task" sheets. The key is not to overburden students with one sheet after another. Keep in mind that we have many different learners within the classroom. What is the ultimate goal? Don't we want to make sure that they "get it?" Then, we must make sure that we are addressing their needs, their ability levels, and their learning styles. If we do not get the outcome we desire, then it is our job to model the skill again in a different way until students are successful and have ownership of the skill. Students need to know that mastering a new skill or strategy may take multiple tries.

APPROXIMATION Along with **PRACTICE,** approximations are also vital. Learning is all about trial and error. Many times we must do something over and over again in order to really "get it." Therefore, students must know this from the very beginning. When students are at the **DISCOVERY** stage of something new, having had multiple attempts will also encourage higher-order thinking. The healthy **ENVIRONMENT** you provide will allow for students to approximate their learning until they have internalized the skill.

SUPPORT As all of the pieces of this formula begin to take shape, support becomes crucial. Support for student learning and mastery comes in many forms. Students can be supported by a peer, a computer, a center, and of course, their teacher. Important to all of this occurring is for the student to know that someone is there to guide, motivate, monitor and coach when, and as often, as the need arises.

RECOGNITION Without any type of recognition, learning and mastery goes by the wayside. Students and adults too, like to know that what they are doing is being noticed, acknowledged, and recognized in some way. Find out what types of recognition your students respond better to. Some like the verbal praise (just make sure that it is specific and genuine), others like the silent nod or wink, some like the pat on the back, a pencil, or lunch with the teacher. Students need to be recognized for their approximations as well as their achievements. Research indicates that recognition is particularly crucial when working with low achievers.

REFLECTIVE PRACTICE. This process helps teachers to recognize themselves as learners. It heightens their awareness as to how their students learn. The teacher should be constantly analyzing the lesson for trouble spots and/or points to re-emphasize. (See **TEACHER'S ROLE**) During, and at the end of your lesson, take a few seconds to check how your lesson went. Was I watching my students? Were they engaged? Did they look confused or puzzled? This reflective act will help you plan for instruction. Then, using reflective practice, continue to utilize strategies resulting in success to the learner and change practice utilizing different teaching strategies for those which have been less than successful. Many teachers find that video taping their lessons enables them to key in to behaviors that may not be evident from recall of the lesson by themselves or a peer coach. Using a videotape, allows the teacher/coach to analyze the lesson in more depth resulting in a deeper understanding of strategies that worked well and those that did not. This reflective act will help you plan for future instruction and enable you to increase student learning outcomes.

   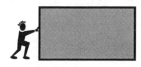

THE FORMULA

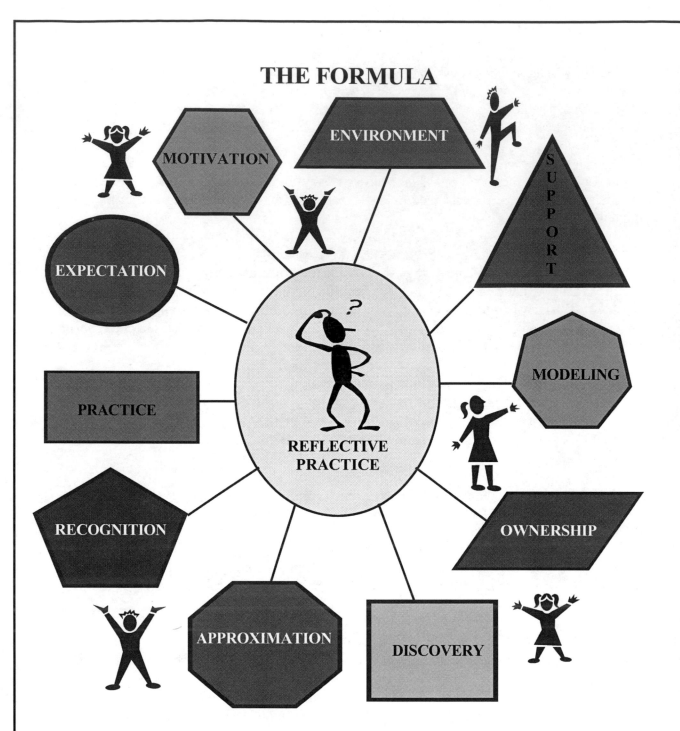

At the center of the "Formula for Success," lies the teacher who sets the stage for learning to occur in the classroom. The learners, all placed around the formula, remind us that all students learn in different ways. Students require different methods of instruction, and a variety of activities, which help them to become lifelong independent learners. Internalizing this formula will enhance your "delivery of instruction," help you run a classroom that is conducive to learning, and create a community of learners as well.

CONFERENCING

Whether you are meeting with students about reading, writing, math, social studies, or science, conferencing is one of the most powerful tools you should have in your classroom. Why? The one-on-one or small group interaction with students helps to build rapport and trust with students. Giving individual attention to each and every student helps to promote self-esteem and confidence. Students begin to lose their fear of sharing their work out loud or being corrected in front of their peers because they know that they will have the support they need in a conference.

It is so much easier just to correct their papers and return them to the students. But as Donald H. Graves (1983) puts it, "correcting is not teaching." The students will never learn if all you do is correct the writing and give it back to them to redo. Students must learn what they are doing incorrectly in a safe setting.

Finding time to conference is easy because it can be part of your reading block, your center time, or even on the spot. Students with the most difficulty should be seen first and often. Most conferences should not last more than 3 or 4 minutes. In some cases, they could even last 30 seconds depending on the student or need.

Conferences should be predictable and focused. Students like routines and procedures. When they know that they will be conferencing at a certain time or day with a particular skill, they will be prepared and thus reduce the amount of time needed at a conference.

How you organize your conference area is an important factor to consider. Sitting next to the students provides a relaxed non-threatening atmosphere. You are in this together, not I am the teacher, and you are the student type of environment that will not allow the student to discuss their piece of writing.

In order to keep conferencing from taking too much time, it is best to limit the conference to one skill or topic of discussion. This will make the conference more focused and not have the student leave more confused than when it started.

Skills can also be taught at conferences. While looking over student work, you may notice a need for a particular skill either with a student or a group of students. Pull all the students together with their writing and model the skill. This skill will become internalized because the students can relate it to their own piece of writing.

Conferencing can also be done with reading strategies. You may conference with students about their fluency while reading, practice with high frequency words, review for a test, or provide comprehension help, etc.

The main goal of conferencing is to make sure that students are getting the immediate feedback they so deserve. Conferencing should involve you asking the questions and the students doing most of the talking. This will enable them to become independent learners.

TYPES OF CONFERENCES

1. **Revising or Editing Conferences.** Students meet with the teacher to correct spelling, punctuation and other mechanics but only one skill at a time. (See **TRAFFIC COURT**.) Revising conferences are about clarifying content, expressing ideas, writing for an audience, author's purpose, or organization. These conferences could take between 20-25 minutes because it involves sharing of writing and discussion. (See **SENTENCE EXTENSION & SENTENCE COMBINING**.)

2. **Purple Penning Conferences** involve the correction of high frequency words from the Word Wall that have been misspelled in writing. When conferencing with a student, the teacher circles or writes **WW** next to a misspelled high frequency word. The student will write it correctly in the margin or bottom of the page. This is non-negotiable!

3. **Mini-Lesson Conferences.** The teacher provides a mini-lesson on a strategy or skill to a student or group of students based on a need seen in writing or a guided reading group. These conferences last only 10 minutes.

4. **Right Here Conferences.** These are the easiest to do because they can happen anywhere. While moving around the room, the teacher notices a student struggling or using a powerful vocabulary word or phrase. The teacher simply stops and asks a couple of questions and moves on not taking more than 2 or 3 minutes.

5. **Drafting Conferences.** Students bring their rough drafts to the conference. This conference involves a little more interaction between the teacher and the student because the student may be stuck with the writing.

6. **Peer Conferences.** Students meet with each other to go over their work. Some students are stronger in editing, drafting, or revising and can help those in need of assistance. Not only does this help the stronger learner, but also helps the teacher meet with all the students.

7. **Whole Class Conferences.** Sometimes it is necessary to hold a whole class conference in order to write, revise, and edit class collaborations. In the same format as the teacher would conduct an individual conference, the teacher asks questions and the students do most of the talking and discussing.

8. **Cloze Conferences** involve students practicing prediction when reading. Students can bring a completed cloze passage to the conference. The teacher can go over the corrections and give feedback on how to think of words that would fill in the blanks.

9. **Guided Reading Conferences** are similar to what happens in a guided reading group but are more personalized. A group of students having the same needs can be brought together for a mini skill lesson.

THE HANDS OF TIME

Harry Wong, *The First Days of School,* suggests that you think about how you are using your time with your students.

ALLOCATED TIME:

This is the amount of time given to student learning. On average it consists of about 6 to 7 hours per day for instructional purposes (scheduled time). It is **100%** of the available time.

INSTRUCTIONAL TIME:

Instructional time is easy to ascertain because the teacher is the focus in the room. It is when an administrator can observe the teacher directing a lesson. Research indicates that teachers are at the center stage in their classrooms **90%** of the allocated time.

ENGAGED TIME:

This is the amount of time your students are "on task" involved in the learning activities aligned with the lesson's objective. The students should be the focus and the teacher should be monitoring student understanding. Students are "engaged" when they are working on the lesson's objective. Research shows that engaged time is about **75%** of the allocated time.

A brief note: If this seems in conflict with instructional time, it is because the teacher and student may be working at the same time.

ACADEMIC LEARNING TIME (ALT)

This is the amount of time that your students are successfully "engaged" in the lesson's objective. Research suggests that this time within the classroom is only **35%** of the allocated time.

The following attributes must be present in order for students to be successful:

1. Did students know and understand the lesson's objective?
2. Are students actively engaged and manipulating the content of the lesson's objective?
3. Can you show that the students learned the objective?
4. Students must be successful 75% of the time (independent learning level).

Students will make the highest achievement marks in classrooms where teachers maximize Academic Learning Time. The rationale behind *Reading and Writing Strategically* is to assist you in increasing the amount of **ALT** and student achievement.

SECTION NOTES

LETTER RECOGNITION

SPELLING

SECTION 2
LANGUAGE DEVELOPMENT

STRATEGIES AND ACTIVITIES

LANGUAGE STATIONS

ENGLISH AS A SECOND LANGUAGE

SPELLING ACQUISITION

As teachers we need to develop a spelling program that begins in the primary grades with active exploration of the letter-sound relationships and progresses through phonics, spelling patterns, the use of high frequency words, and word usage. Why? Spelling is for writing, not reading. Spelling is really word study, or a way in which students discover and examine regularities, patterns, and the rules of orthography needed to read and spell.

There is a considerable correlation between spelling achievement and reading achievement. We need to link our spelling to a balanced literacy approach. This can be accomplished through a reading and writing program that has students working in their "Zone of Proximal Development" (Vygotsky, 1962). Even though a student can read a particular word, that word may not necessarily be an appropriate one for a spelling list. This is due to the fact that a student's reading vocabulary may be more extensive than their writing vocabulary.

By using regular student assessments and observations, you will be able to track your students' progress and development. You may be required to give spelling grades, or spelling may be part of an overall language arts grade. Your school district's curriculum guidelines should be able to assist you in coming up with a word list. Ideally, a spelling grade should not consist of only an average on a Friday assessment. One way to obtain spelling words for use in your spelling program is to monitor writing samples. Simply look for misspellings in student writing and make them part of your spelling list. (See **1000 HIGH FREQUENCY WORDS, WORD WALLS, WORD WALL ACTIVITY MATRIX, & MAKING WORDS**.)

The activities referenced above in blue can also be used as an alternative means of assessing spelling. Active participation in **Making Words**, having materials ready, and completing weekly **Word Wall Matrix** activities all lend themselves to hands-on, engaging learning opportunities for children.

HANDWRITING

"I can't read it!" Complains a teacher. Our first response is, "Are you requiring your students to use cursive handwriting?" Far too often, we insist that our students demonstrate their best handwriting. How unrealistic! Do you not draft "sloppy copies" at times? However, there are times when legibility is important. Our goal as teachers should be to help our students to develop and use legible handwriting to communicate in their writing. How often do you use cursive? On the computer, or filling out a form? No! We need to de-emphasize cursive handwriting, and understand that our main concern when evaluating a piece of writing is to focus on content rather than neatness. By doing so, we will help to foster better attitudes in students towards their own writing.

MAKING WORDS
THEORY AND RESEARCH

Making Words, developed by Cunningham and Cunningham (1992), is an active, hands-on activity. Students try to make up as many words as they can, when given a set of letters that will eventually make up a word. Beginning with two-letter words, students make between 15 and 20 words in the allotted time, finally coming up with the big word. Students are given a letter strip where they write down all the letters, vowels first, followed by consonants in alphabetical order. Writing down the vowels in **red** will highlight that all words have vowels in them.

Making Words lessons should not last more than 20 minutes. Lessons lasting any longer can cause frustration or boredom among some students. This activity is designed to be fast-paced, engaging, and fun! Through manipulating letters, students discover letter-sound relationships, patterns, little words within big words, etc. They even notice that by adding a letter to an already existing pattern or rearranging a word, they have just made a new word.

After students have been given enough time to play with words, the teacher will help them sort for patterns using a pocket chart. Words can also be sorted for prefixes, suffixes, and common endings, etc.

You will notice a marked increase in their spelling and writing because Making Words transfers over to reading, spelling, and writing.

PLANNING A MAKING WORDS LESSON

* ❖ Decide what your final word will be. Think about your students and their abilities. Pick a word that will challenge all of your students but not frustrate them. For further impact, choose a word that is content related!
* ❖ Using 3 x 5 index cards, write down as many of the words that you would like for the students to make.
* ❖ From the words you have chosen, (15-20), pick the ones that can be sorted by patterns, common beginnings, endings, blends, and vowel combinations. Include a few proper nouns so they practice seeing where capital letters belong.
* ❖ Sort all of these words from shortest to longest and then again by patterns and commonalities.
* ❖ Write the big word on one side of the index card and the sort patterns on the back.
* ❖ Make sure that you have plenty of letter strips or individual letters for each student. This is the **most important step** to Making Words. Students must have their own letters to manipulate.
* ❖ You need to have a pocket chart or something to display the letters and words you are working with. **Remember!** This is a visual, hands-on activity!

STEPS IN TEACHING A MAKING WORDS LESSON

1. Place the large letters for your word in a pocket chart. Vowels first, followed by consonants in alphabetical order.

2. Provide each student with a letter strip. Letters are then copied in the exact order in which they are displayed and then cut out. Remember, vowels in **red!**

3. Students are given a few minutes (5-7), to try and write down as many two-letter, three-letter, four-letter words, etc. they can in the time provided. (See **MAKING WORDS CENTER ACTIVITY**.)

4. With the index cards previously prepared, use a two-letter word in a sentence as students make the word with their own letters. Circulate around the room to check that students are correctly spelling these words. Give the word card to one student to place in the pocket chart.

5. Continue having students make the words on your cards. Cue them when it is time to change one letter or two in order to make a new word. It is also important to let students know when you may be pronouncing a homophone. As they get better, students will ask you which homophone you are referring to.

6. Once all the words have been made and are on the pocket chart, proceed to sorting. These words can be sorted by prefixes, common beginnings, vowel combinations, or blends. The more you do this activity, the better your students will get. We have noticed, that after a few times, they will automatically sort the words as they place them in the pocket chart.

7. If students have not come up with the big word until now, give them clues to how the word may start or end, a definition or a synonym.

8. Another activity with Making Words is transfer words. The students will not have all the letters for these words but will begin to see that adding a letter or two to their existing letters will form many more words. The words should have a "T" marked on the index card for your reference.

9. Making Words Works!!!!! The more you do it, the better they get at it!

10. Making Words lessons can be modified for primary and intermediate grades and more difficult for middle and high school. (See **REFERENCES**.)

**In order to see results and transfer of skills to reading and writing,
Making Words should be done at least three times a week.**

MAKING WORDS LETTER STRIPS

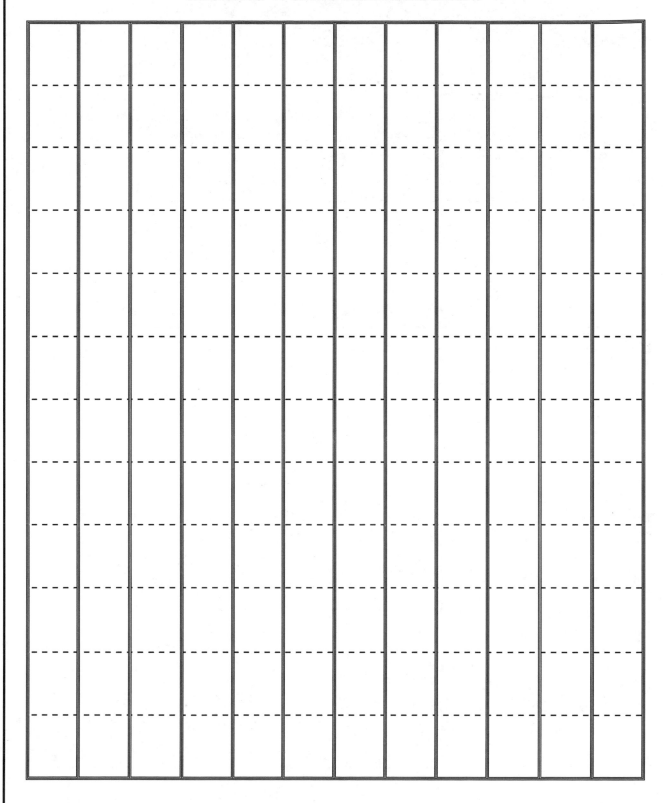

MAKING WORDS CENTER ACTIVITY

DIRECTIONS:
Students find words for the jumbled letters and list them in the appropriate column. They should remember to double-check the spelling of each word using classroom resources. A dictionary, spell checker, or a classmate can assist them in this process. Transfer words are words for which they will need to add a letter or two (affixes) to their existing letters in order to make another word. Challenge students to set personal goals for the number of words they can discover for each column!

2 LETTER WORDS	3 LETTER WORDS	4 LETTER WORDS	5 LETTER WORDS	6 LETTER WORDS	7 LETTER WORDS

8 LETTER WORDS	9 LETTER WORDS	10 LETTER WORDS	11 LETTER WORDS	12 LETTER WORDS	TRANSFER WORDS

Two other similar types of activities are **Anagrams** and the electronic hand-held game, **Hangman**.

HIGH FREQUENCY WORDS

There are just some words that you do not want students to have to decode while reading, or invent the spelling of while writing! Those words are the words that are frequently found in our language.

When students learn to recognize these high frequency words and automatically spell them, their attention is freed up for decoding and spelling the less-frequent words, and, more important, for understanding what they are reading. This also transfers over to writing. Students are able to add richer vocabulary to their writing when they can write a first draft spelling the high frequency words correctly. More time can be spent enhancing the piece of writing instead of correcting high frequency words, sometimes causing extreme frustration among writers.

Learning these high frequency words is not always easy because so many of them are not pronounced or spelled in predictable ways. Many of the words cannot be decoded. Most of the words are functional, connecting abstract words that have no meaning in and of themselves. Therefore, it is vital that students practice these words over and over again, in a **variety of ways**, and **often**!

It is important to provide a way for students to associate meaning with the words. Students can also be taught to find a word they know within the word or a word that rhymes with that word, in order to remember it. If a common word has many confusable words, teach one first. Once that word is mastered teach the second one. When the second one is mastered, practice them both, and so on.

We have included the 1000 most frequently used words 95% of the time in writing. The **Daytona 500** are meant for the primary and intermediate grades. A first grade teacher may want to concentrate on the 1st 40, a 2nd grade teacher would overlap up to 80, and so on. **The Last Lap**, or last 500 words are meant for the upper grades. From here on in, they will be referred to as the **1000 High Frequency Words**. They are only meant as a starting point! Looking through students' writing is the ideal opportunity to find commonly misspelled high frequency words. The goal is to have all students spelling these high frequency words correctly while writing.

STARTING POINT

FINISH LINE

THE DAYTONA 500

1.	the	47.	had	93.	its
2.	of	48.	when	94.	find
3.	and	49.	each	95.	day
4.	a	50.	not	96.	made
5.	to	51.	will	97.	long
6.	it	52.	out	98.	come
7.	in	53.	then	99.	part
8.	you	54.	her	100.	down
9.	that	55.	into	101.	over
10.	he	56.	has	102.	only
11.	was	57.	look	103.	years
12.	on	58.	two	104.	most
13.	with	59.	more	105.	back
14.	I	60.	go	106.	things
15.	at	61.	see	107.	our
16.	be	62.	up	108.	just
17.	this	63.	other	109.	name
18.	is	64.	like	110.	good
19.	for	65.	him	111.	am
20.	are	66.	about	112.	new
21.	have	67.	many	113.	sound
22.	as	68.	them	114.	take
23.	his	69.	these	115.	place
24.	they	70.	so	116.	me
25.	from	71.	some	117.	give
26.	do	72.	would	118.	after
27.	all	73.	make	119.	little
28.	were	74.	time	120.	work
29.	which	75.	write	121.	know
30.	she	76.	no	122.	live
31.	or	77.	my	123.	very
32.	one	78.	who	124.	man
33.	by	79.	six	125.	think
34.	word	80.	get	126.	say
35.	but	81.	did	127.	help
36.	we	82.	may	128.	before
37.	there	83.	how	129.	too
38.	use	84.	than	130.	old
39.	an	85.	yes	131.	tell
40.	if	86.	way	132.	came
41.	their	87.	could	133.	also
42.	now	88.	people	134.	three
43.	said	89.	first	135.	great
44.	your	90.	water	136.	where
45.	can	91.	been	137.	much
46.	what	92.	called	138.	any

THE DAYTONA 500

139. through	185. change	231. life
140. line	186. page	232. got
141. right	187. answer	233. run
142. means	188. found	234. those
143. small	189. study	235. both
144. same	190. picture	236. along
145. boy	191. play	237. close
146. cat	192. spell	238. don't
147. want	193. air	239. hard
148. show	194. away	240. beginning
149. around	195. point	241. always
150. form	196. mother	242. paper
151. men	197. animals	243. together
152. went	198. house	244. group
153. home	199. should	245. often
154. us	200. brother	246. while
155. end	201. high	247. might
156. well	202. city	248. something
157. must	203. under	249. example
158. need	204. head	250. seemed
159. big	205. eyes	251. side
160. read	206. father	252. feet
161. land	207. keep	253. car
162. move	208. own	254. four
163. set	209. last	255. once
164. put	210. near	256. book
165. does	211. food	257. stop
166. large	212. below	258. later
167. even	213. never	259. until
168. such	214. every	260. night
169. here	215. add	261. sea
170. asked	216. between	262. grow
171. different	217. country	263. carry
172. turned	218. plants	264. hear
173. another	219. school	265. important
174. because	220. trees	266. children
175. why	221. started	267. miles
176. try	222. earth	268. walked
177. off	223. light	269. river
178. again	224. thought	270. white
179. letters	225. story	271. began
180. still	226. saw	272. without
181. learn	227. left	273. second
182. world	228. few	274. took
183. hand	229. next	275. state
184. kind	230. open	276. miss

THE DAYTONA 500

277.	far	323.	remember	369.	seen
278.	let	324.	easy	370.	sing
279.	list	325.	however	371.	town
280.	leave	326.	best	372.	field
281.	it's	327.	birds	373.	upon
282.	idea	328.	questions	374.	wind
283.	eat	329.	stand	375.	fast
284.	girl	330.	become	376.	toward
285.	young	331.	ship	377.	passed
286.	talk	332.	music	378.	table
287.	song	333.	mark	379.	money
288.	face	334.	problem	380.	voice
289.	enough	335.	knew	381.	ground
290.	almost	336.	door	382.	unit
291.	hot	337.	today	383.	wood
292.	mountains	338.	complete	384.	rock
293.	cut	339.	during	385.	covered
294.	soon	340.	told	386.	several
295.	being	341.	heard	387.	morning
296.	family	342.	waves	388.	numeral
297.	really	343.	products	389.	slowly
298.	Indians	344.	happened	390.	pulled
299.	above	345.	usually	391.	cold
300.	watch	346.	reached	392.	cried
301.	body	347.	didn't	393.	notice
302.	low	348.	early	394.	king
303.	room	349.	measure	395.	figure
304.	top	350.	hours	396.	travel
305.	area	351.	five	397.	hold
306.	sun	352.	true	398.	himself
307.	red	353.	north	399.	vowel
308.	since	354.	draw	400.	against
309.	whole	355.	plan	401.	ten
310.	friends	356.	south	402.	box
311.	better	357.	war	403.	oh
312.	dog	358.	fall	404.	feel
313.	fish	359.	I'll	405.	note
314.	sure	360.	certain	406.	rest
315.	across	361.	fire	407.	green
316.	color	362.	listen	408.	week
317.	order	363.	space	409.	ago
318.	ever	364.	step	410.	ran
319.	black	365.	hundred	411.	game
320.	short	366.	pattern	412.	warm
321.	horse	367.	map	413.	dry
322.	piece	368.	farm	414.	number

THE DAYTONA 500

415.	yet	461.	half
416.	heat	462.	finally
417.	sentence	463.	correct
418.	oil	464.	became
419.	less	465.	base
420.	ball	466.	decided
421.	fine	467.	surface
422.	done	468.	nothing
423.	fly	469.	wheels
424.	wait	470.	understand
425.	front	471.	behind
426.	ocean	472.	system
427.	stay	473.	though
428.	known	474.	language
429.	stood	475.	object
430.	boat	476.	rule
431.	brought	477.	able
432.	deep	478.	material
433.	clear	479.	built
434.	round	480.	quickly
435.	full	481.	shown
436.	sometimes	482.	minutes
437.	power	483.	stars
438.	dark	484.	contain
439.	road	485.	produce
440.	gave	486.	carefully
441.	person	487.	government
442.	strong	488.	plane
443.	fact	489.	equation
444.	street	490.	shape
445.	course	491.	thousands
446.	class	492.	noun
447.	inside	493.	cannot
448.	island	494.	special
449.	machine	495.	pair
450.	force	496.	include
451.	common	497.	verb
452.	bring	498.	inches
453.	explain	499.	building
454.	filled	500.	scientists
455.	check		
456.	among		
457.	size		
458.	heavy		
459.	circle		
460.	English		

THE LAST LAP

501. can't	547. whether	593. members
502. test	548. shall	594. developed
503. center	549. held	595. distance
504. anything	550. drive	596. probably
505. ready	551. square	597. reason
506. love	552. suddenly	598. present
507. rain	553. farmers	599. root
508. blue	554. general	600. months
509. drop	555. moon	601. son
510. sit	556. believe	602. ice
511. forest	557. picked	603. ride
512. sat	558. paint	604. floor
513. wide	559. eggs	605. buy
514. kept	560. window	606. tall
515. race	561. summer	607. bed
516. job	562. legs	608. copy
517. sign	563. written	609. free
518. wild	564. American	610. hope
519. happy	565. beautiful	611. case
520. gone	566. edge	612. type
521. west	567. record	613. lead
522. meet	568. beside	614. lake
523. soft	569. glass	615. hair
524. flowers	570. lay	616. age
525. teacher	571. paragraph	617. tiny
526. bill	572. clothes	618. gold
527. felt	573. describe	619. milk
528. direction	574. matter	620. quiet
529. energy	575. perhaps	621. lot
530. return	576. divided	622. build
531. dance	577. subject	623. following
532. simple	578. cells	624. sail
533. cause	579. mind	625. bear
534. wish	580. exercise	626. trip
535. heart	581. train	627. poor
536. sum	582. difference	628. let's
537. wall	583. winter	629. died
538. main	584. length	630. dress
539. arms	585. interest	631. cross
540. store	586. discovered	632. speak
541. past	587. million	633. sleep
542. finished	588. instruments	634. snow
543. sky	589. represent	635. hill
544. weather	590. syllables	636. baby
545. third	591. Europe	637. soil
546. raised	592. region	638. spring

THE LAST LAP

639. quite	685. century	731. party
640. within	686. everything	732. woman
641. amount	687. instead	733. bank
642. broken	688. phrase	734. choose
643. natural	689. nation	735. clean
644. act	690. temperature	736. visit
645. count	691. method	737. whose
646. smiled	692. consonant	738. garden
647. killed	693. dictionary	739. please
648. hole	694. although	740. strange
649. fight	695. per	741. caught
650. beat	696. moment	742. fell
651. remain	697. fraction	743. team
652. iron	698. Africa	744. God
653. fingers	699. bottom	745. captain
654. solve	700. French	746. ring
655. appear	701. row	747. child
656. metal	702. least	748. cost
657. either	703. catch	749. maybe
658. village	704. wrote	750. break
659. factors	705. else	751. uncle
660. care	706. gas	752. flow
661. pushed	707. design	753. lady
662. outside	708. foot	754. art
663. already	709. law	755. climbed
664. laughed	710. ears	756. shouted
665. themselves	711. you're	757. plains
666. bright	712. skin	758. England
667. everyone	713. key	759. joined
668. section	714. brown	760. grass
669. scale	715. cool	761. grew
670. pounds	716. lost	762. president
671. possible	717. sent	763. trouble
672. stone	718. wear	764. cloud
673. middle	719. save	765. bad
674. speed	720. engine	766. drawing
675. someone	721. alone	767. touch
676. rolled	722. east	768. equal
677. wonder	723. pay	769. practice
678. angle	724. single	770. report
679. melody	725. mouth	771. statement
680. surprise	726. yard	772. seeds
681. exactly	727. yourself	773. suppose
682. couldn't	728. control	774. coast
683. result	729. rise	775. wire
684. jumped	730. stick	776. bit

THE LAST LAP

777. received	823. rich	869. tone
778. direct	824. chief	870. provide
779. serve	825. eight	871. tail
780. desert	826. major	872. compound
781. increase	827. army	873. belong
782. history	828. hat	874. compare
783. business	829. swim	875. elements
784. separate	830. park	876. indicate
785. hunting	831. wash	877. expect
786. students	832. wife	878. sense
787. feeling	833. supply	879. value
788. continued	834. crops	880. movement
789. itself	835. thus	881. exciting
790. burning	836. won't	882. branches
791. valley	837. bones	883. lie
792. cents	838. modern	884. suggested
793. symbols	839. addition	885. entered
794. experiment	840. soldiers	886. tied
795. information	841. guess	887. send
796. express	842. trade	888. Japanese
797. decimal	843. rather	889. planets
798. straight	844. crowd	890. science
799. period	845. interesting	891. tube
800. human	846. string	892. weight
801. hit	847. famous	893. lifted
802. sand	848. pole	894. property
803. doctor	849. blood	895. particular
804. cook	850. spot	896. current
805. board	851. consider	897. shoulder
806. mine	852. position	898. industry
807. wasn't	853. fruit	899. sharp
808. fit	854. dollars	900. insects
809. safe	855. sight	901. radio
810. silent	856. stream	902. we'll
811. poem	857. rhythm	903. action
812. enjoy	858. observe	904. yellow
813. except	859. necessary	905. isn't
814. flat	860. meat	906. truck
815. seven	861. process	907. fair
816. blow	862. terms	908. wouldn't
817. wings	863. sell	909. chance
818. thick	864. block	910. level
819. bell	865. spread	911. sister
820. fun	866. cattle	912. chart
821. loud	867. corner	913. pretty
822. thin	868. electric	914. shop

THE LAST LAP

915.	shoes	961.	fig
916.	nose	962.	huge
917.	afraid	963.	similar
918.	dead	964.	score
919.	sugar	965.	experience
920.	office	966.	workers
921.	gun	967.	women
922.	death	968.	northern
923.	stretched	969.	difficult
924.	rose	970.	steel
925.	fear	971.	deal
926.	led	972.	evening
927.	march	973.	details
928.	create	974.	entire
929.	match	975.	substances
930.	win	976.	smell
931.	doesn't	977.	conditions
932.	total	978.	track
933.	rope	979.	arrived
934.	cotton	980.	sir
935.	apple	981.	effect
936.	corn	982.	underline
937.	tools	983.	factories
938.	cows	984.	southern
939.	located	985.	molecules
940.	seat	986.	France
941.	division	987.	column
942.	view	988.	various
943.	company	989.	prepared
944.	capital	990.	solution
945.	settled	991.	suffix
946.	printed	992.	forward
947.	ahead	993.	Washington
948.	born	994.	Greek
949.	triangle	995.	bought
950.	repeated	996.	British
951.	western	997.	determine
952.	church	998.	nor
953.	oxygen	999.	opposite
954.	plural	1000.	allow
955.	agreed		
956.	wrong		
957.	fresh		
958.	especially		
959.	actually		
960.	adjective		

WORD WALLS

Word Walls or Words on the Wall (Cunningham, Moore, 1989) is a strategy that helps to teach high frequency or commonly occurring words. The Word Wall is a place in the room that is visible by all students. Words are added on a weekly basis. Depending on your students, three to five words will be added a week for primary, and seven to ten for intermediate. The goal is not to just add the words but **use** the wall on a daily basis to reinforce the high frequency words. Teachers and students work collaboratively to choose the words that will go on the wall from their writing. Students practice spelling patterns, decoding strategies, and word meanings and purposes within the context of real reading and writing. **Word Walls are not for vocabulary words.**

Why use Word Walls?

Word Walls are constant visual reminders to students that the words on the wall must be spelled correctly all of the time, since they are in plain sight. To further enhance the effectiveness of this strategy, make an individual Word Wall Folder for each student. (See sample **Word Wall Folder**.) Words will then be spelled correctly no matter where they are: home, other classrooms, or in a different setting altogether.

What does a Word Wall look like?

A Word Wall has all of the letters of the alphabet. Underneath the alphabet, words are written big enough for all students to see. Words can be framed cut, chunks underlined, blends written in the same color, vowels in one color, and consonants in another. You will need to adjust how you write these words with the grade level you are teaching. The main thing to remember is that this is a working Word Wall. If the students cannot see the word, they will not spell it correctly. If necessary, take something else down in your room in order to make room for a Word Wall.

Where does the Word Wall fit into my daily schedule?

Word work should last no more than 15 minutes daily. It should be a natural extension of your shared or guided reading and writing. Keep the words you are working on for the week in one location. On a daily basis, do some kind of activity with your words. (See **WORD WALL ACTIVITY MATRIX**.) At the end of the week, add these words to your wall.

How long do the words stay up?

A Word Wall is a work in progress. Once you notice that the majority of your students are spelling a word correctly all of the time, take it down! Students will feel a sense of accomplishment because they are finally using the word correctly. Since students have their own personal Word Wall, they will still have that word for reference, should they need it. If you have an **Editor's Spot** in your room with a display board that doubles as a Mini-Word Wall, students will have the word for reference while writing.

STEPS FOR SUCCESSFUL WORD WALLS

1. **Students need to be involved**. You and your students build Word Walls. Tell your students why you have a Word Wall up. Let them help you come up with the words that go up on the wall.

2. **Word selection.** Select words that you see commonly misspelled in their daily work or words that have irregular spelling and do not follow a pattern.

3. **Make use of the Word Wall automatic.** It should be a part of your daily routine.

4. **Practice for the Word Wall words should be engaging, active, and meaningful.** Writing words five times each does not help students learn how to spell a word correctly if they are practicing it wrong! (See **WORD WALL ACTIVITY MATRIX**.)

5. **All eyes should be on the Word Wall.** When doing daily activities with the words, students' eyes should be focused on the Word Wall. Words are visible, bold, attractive, and neat.

6. **Number of words.** The number of words selected will vary according to the grade you teach and your students' needs.

7. **Take words down.** A cluttered word wall is an ineffective Word Wall. Words should be taken down when most of your students spell that word correctly all of the time.

8. **Location.** Have a place in the room where students can manipulate the Word Wall words. The more hands-on activities provided with the words, the quicker they will internalize the words and take ownership of them.

9. **Practice word families.** When students see the connections between words, they become better readers and writers.

10. **Words within words.** Teach students to find the little words within words. Students will begin to see that some of the big words they cannot decode are only made up of little words.

WORD WALL FOLDER

A	B	C	D	E

F	G	H	I	J

Using a file folder sectioned off as seen above, students are in charge of writing their weekly Word Wall words. This enables the students to take their words wherever they go. It is a good idea to periodically check these for correct spelling of words. Below you will see what a Word Wall folder may look like a few weeks into the school year.

K	L	M	N	O
keep	like laugh little	many more	never now no	open off our

P	Q	R	S	T
people	quiet	right really	said school	too then

WORD WALL ACTIVITY MATRIX

Before students begin this activity, have them staple two sheets of lined writing paper to the back of this paper. They will be using this sheet, along with their writing paper, throughout the week as they select a different activity each day to complete using this week's Word Wall Words. All three sheets stapled together, along with the matrix, will be turned in at the end of the week.

Place this week's Word Wall Words in alphabetical order.	**Using the letters in your name, make as many words as you can.**	**Pick a partner and spell this week's words as fast as you can. Record your time _____ and the number correct _____**
Write your Word Wall Words using **BLACK** for consonants and **RED** for vowels.	**SELF-SELECTED CHOICE** **(Teacher approval required)**	**Find synonyms and antonyms for each of your words.** Challenge yourself to find homographs and homophones also.
Draw word frames around each Word Wall Word. **Example:** second	**Find small words within words throughout the classroom.** **Example:** 'all' in small	**Beside each of your Word Wall Words write a rhyming word.**

PARTNER SPELLING

This activity can be modified for any group of students. All you will need to do is pull a group of words from the **1000 High Frequency Words**. For primary aged children, you will use the lower numbered words, and conversely, for middle and high school students, pull words with higher numbers. We usually have four sets of twenty, 3 x 5 index cards, set aside and rubber banded together, allowing a number of students to practice their spelling throughout the room. They can also interchange groups of cards for more practice.

The reason we have chosen these words? They are most likely the words your students are using in their writing. Remember, spelling is for writing!

Instruct students to work with a quiet voice level. Paper and a pencil may be required of those students who are visual in nature. Let them write their words on scratch paper. The goal is for students to spell as many words correctly as possible, and record their results on a clipboard.

With a partner, students will alternate turns after each word. We do not want our students to spell all twenty words at a time, and then ask their partner to spell the words they are holding. If a student misspells a word, allow them a second chance. If a student gets it wrong on the second attempt, it is time to alternate turns.

We teach our students this strategy:

❖ For every word spelled correctly, they place that card down on their right side.

❖ For each word they spell incorrectly, they place that card down on their left side.

This allows the student to quickly count up the number of cards they spelled correctly, or count up the words they misspelled and subtract that number from twenty. Oops! We just integrated math!

38

LIANNE'S LANGUAGE LINK

Lianne's Language Link will help you introduce unfamiliar words or vocabulary to students before a unit of study. Even words associated with each other (but not necessarily in their reading assignment) help to build background knowledge. It is an adaptation of the game *Rivet*, developed by Patricia M. Cunningham, which has all of the student's eyes riveted to the area of the room as the teacher slowly reveals each letter of a word.

Often when children read, they come across many words they have never seen before. This creates unrest in many children, even ourselves. When faced with a new word, what good reader strategies do we employ? Good readers look at all the letters of the word, in sequence. Struggling readers sometimes glance over words that they have trouble reading, without looking for patterns, affixes, base words, or words that are similar. Lianne's Language Link will get your students to pay close attention to these patterns and discover new words!

Choose anywhere from 7 – 10 vocabulary words about what you are going to study next. Write numbers and dashed lines on the overhead (or use a pocket chart) to indicate how many letters each word has. Students should copy this information onto their paper, or for better results, have a universal sheet of paper for each student to use for this activity. (See below.)

Display the first letter of the first word. Continue to display one new letter of the first word until students think they know the word. Many students will guess, not paying attention to spelling patterns. When they give you an incorrect response, continue to display one more letter until someone guesses the correct word. As they become more proficient, their guesses will be much better and it will take fewer letters displayed for them to guess the word. You can also display the common letter in all of the words, as another variation.

Once the word has been guessed correctly, ask the student to finish spelling it. Continue in this fashion until all the words have been correctly guessed and spelled.

LIANNE'S TEMPLATE

1.											
2.											
3.											
4.											
5.											

WENDELL'S WITTY WORDS

Have you ever played Wheel of Fortune? Well, Wendell's Witty Words is an adaptation of the nightly game show and an easily adaptable extension of **Lianne's Language Link**.

To play the game, categories must be prepared. Categories we have used include many from the TV game itself: phrases, places, people, before and after, and landmarks, just to name a few. Additionally, the use of a pocket chart helps for the visualization effects!

Before you begin playing Wendell's Witty Words we suggest that your students watch a little television. Your students can learn a number of strategies by having them watch contestants play the game. For instance: the consonants R, S, T, L, and N are frequently selected first, and vowels usually called later in the round.

Since the number of spaces will be displayed on the pocket chart for the given category, students will have some visual clues about the length of words. As a rule, we do not allow vowels to be called until most of the consonants have been identified. In doing so, this helps students identify consonant clusters, prefixes, and spaces for possible vowel digraphs.

It will be extremely important that you take on the role of Pat Sajak to moderate this activity. As in **Lianne's Language Link**, a prepared piece of paper for all of your students to fill out as the game progresses is important. (See below.) As a letter is chosen, simply turn over the letter called on the pocket chart. If there is more than one of the same letter, all are displayed.

When a student believes that they know the answer, they must fill out their sheet with the words spelled correctly. If a student knows the answer, but cannot spell all of it, they may need to wait until more letters are displayed. This game incorporates knowledge about a subject, and spelling connections.

Since your students are **Making Words** on a regular basis, they will be able to compete and play Wendell's Witty Words rather easily.

WENDELL'S TEMPLATE

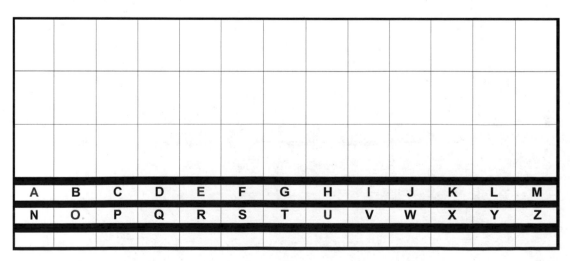

ACROSS, DOWN, OR DIAGONALLY

It has taken us quite some time to come up with another way in which our students can use, learn, and manipulate the high-frequency words that they so desperately need to spell correctly in their writing. We firmly believe, even though this requires quite a lot of preparation time on the teacher's part, that your students will truly be engaged with this activity. It is a game that we implemented after the first grading period and our Word Wall was established with an ample amount of words.

We used words from the **1000 High Frequency Words** and 3 x 5 index cards. On one side of the card you write synonyms, antonyms, a definition, a homophone, in combination or separately. Use just enough of a clue about the word. On the opposite side of the index card write the word you have written the clue for. Continue to do this, but only use the words that have previously been Word Wall Words and are displayed on your Word Wall.

Here is the tricky part. We modified a small pocket chart using strategically placed brads to hold the cards in place. The chart is set up like a bingo card with a free space in the center location. We also divided up the alphabet into chunks for section headings: A-E, F-J, K-O, P-T, and U-Z. Using different colored index cards for each section helps to keep this activity organized and makes it visually appealing too!

Two students take turns trying to identify the word using the clues, and then spelling the word correctly. They must spell the word correctly in order for the card to count as one of the five in a row.

This is an example of one index card:

FRONT	**BACK**
(visible to student)	**(hidden from view)**

| 5   2   H

Syn: joyous, merry, glad

Ant: blue, gloomy, sad | **happy** |

By now you are wondering why the 5, 2, and H are written on the front of the card. They are clues for the students. The word is five letters long, has two syllables, and begins with the letter H.

For more information, please see **www.readingandwritingstrategically.com** where we have photographs of this activity.

COMMON ROOTS AND AFFIXES

Many students stumble or skip over big words when they are reading and avoid using them when writing, causing this to be the most common reading and spelling problem for older students. These words are made up of roots and affixes or morphemic units.

Once students are taught some of the most common roots and affixes, they will start seeing them while reading. They are then empowered with the skill of being able to pronounce and sometimes even learn the meanings of the words they used to skip over.

Example:

Create is what you do.
A creator is the person doing it.
The creation is what you have once you have created.

More proficient readers and writers are able to explore the Greek and Latin word roots from which many words in the English language are constructed. In reading, this extra knowledge makes it possible to decode polysyllabic words at a fairly sophisticated level.

Roots sometimes help to come up with meanings of words. Roots and their meanings must be taught so that students can see how many words in that family are related.

port = reporter, portable, export

The spelling-meaning connection provides the opportunity to help students learn a strategy for examining words that are related in spelling and meaning as well as to help them become aware of the several different spelling-meaning patterns that characterize so many words in English.

Greek and Latin word roots form a large part of the new vocabulary that students encounter in the intermediate years and beyond. These roots cannot stand alone.

Greek and Latin roots should be introduced according to the abstractness of their meaning, from concrete to the more abstract. For example, the Greek roots *phon* (sound), *auto* (self) and the Latin roots *spect* (to look), *rupt* (to break, burst) are introduced and explored early.

Teach about words in meaning "families." This highlights the awareness that particular patterns and relationships can be extended or generalized to other words. There needs to be a balance of teacher-directed instruction with students' investigations and discussions.

On the next page are a few common roots and affixes. They have been put in bookmark form for students to keep handy as they study our complex English language.

COMMON ROOTS AND AFFIXES BOOKMARKS

GREEK	LATIN	PREFIXES	SUFFIXES
auto: (self) autograph	**aud**: (to hear) audible	**anti**: (against) antislavery	**able:** (inclined to) agreeable
bio: (life) biology	**cred**: (to believe) credible	**bi**: (two) bicycle	**ed**: (past-tense verbs) talked
chron: (time) chronic	**dict**: (to say) dictate	**dis**: (not) dislike	**ent**: (one who) resident
gram: (thing written) diagram	**duc(t)**: (to lead) introduce, deduct	**en/em**: (in, into, cover) engage, employ	**er:** (one who) teacher
hydr: (water) hydrant	**flec/flex**: (to bend) reflection, flexible	**in**: (into, not) include	**est**: (most) smartest
hyper: (over, above) hypercritical	**form**: (shape) formation	**mis**: (not) mistake	**ful**: (full of) flavorful
logo: (word, reason) logic	**fract**: (to break) fraction	**non**: (not) nonsense	**ive**: (adjective form of a noun) active
micro: (small) microscope	**ject**: (throw) reject	**pre**: (before) pretest	**ion/tion**: (state of) perfection
phil: (love) philosophy	**jud**: (judge) judgment	**pro**: (in favor of) protest	**ly**: (every) weekly
phon: (sound) telephone	**port**: (to carry) import	**re**: (again) return	**less**: (without) fatherless, penniless
photo: (light) photography	**rupt**: (to break) disrupt	**sub**: (under, beneath) submarine	**ment**: (action or process) involvement
scope: (instrument for viewing) telescope	**scrib/script**: (to write) describe, transcript	**super**: (above, beyond) superior	**ness**: (state of being) weakness
techn: (art, skill, craft) technical	**sect/sec**: (cut) intersect, midsection	**tele**: (far) telephone	**ology**: (study of) biology
therm: (heat) thermometer	**spect**: (to look) inspect	**tri**: (three) triangle	**s/es**: (plurals) walks, watches
zoo: (animal) zoology	**tang/tact**: (to touch) tangible	**un**: (not) unknown	**y**: (state of) shiny
		under: (beneath, below) underline	
		uni: (one) unicycle	

SECTION NOTES

LISTENING STATIONS

FUNCTIONAL READING

SECTION 3
READING COMPREHENSION

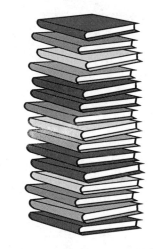

STRATEGIES & ACTIVITIES

COOPERATIVE GROUPS

READING FOR ENJOYMENT

INSTILLING THE LOVE OF READING

This section of our book is devoted to instilling the love of reading in our students by using a period of time devoted solely for reading enjoyment. After all do you not have a favorite author that you just love to sit and read? Research is inconclusive on whether or not this practice increases fluency, creates better readers, or has better readers just simply reading more. Due to this, we would like to suggest possible ways of turning students' apathy towards reading into an intrinsic desire to read, and create a feeling of self-satisfaction after reading.

A program that promotes self-selected reading materials on a student's independent reading level might include:

- ❖ An environment that promotes choices for reading enjoyment.
- ❖ Students could follow the rule of 5 (no more than 5 miscues per page).
- ❖ Classroom libraries with at least 400-500 titles with varying readability levels.
- ❖ Books that are of high interest and engaging must be part of the classroom library.
- ❖ Comics, newspapers, picture books, magazines, and novels should be available.

Two fundamental purposes of having students read independently are for them to build vocabulary and develop reading fluency. In order for this to be accomplished, children must learn 3000—4000 words per year to be reading on grade level. For automaticity, children need to experience words in text 4 to 14 times successfully. Did your parents read the same book over and over to you?

The teacher's role is to first model how to choose appropriately leveled text that will not cause frustration while reading silently. Selections can be monitored as you circulate around the room and you have them read a paragraph or two, when you tap them on the shoulder. You can monitor student progress by keeping a log of how each student is reading. At this time, record how the student is reading, monitor the rule of 5, make suggestions, and guide the student into appropriately leveled books. Students will sometimes choose a book that "looks" right but is not on their independent level and is much too difficult for them to read.

During independent reading, students like to practice applying and demonstrating good reader strategies that you have modeled. Reading fluently, adjusting pace and voice intonations, and using punctuation gives the students confidence. Predicting, confirming, re-reading, and self-correcting, maintaining meaning, and being able to summarize are all strategies that help to aid in comprehension. (See **RECIPROCAL TEACHING**.)

Think about how your classroom is arranged. Do you allow students to use all available space within the classroom? However, be careful with the amount of time it takes students to find their little nook or empty space. It is important to use all the allotted time for the purpose of reading.

At the end of independent reading time, you might consider the use of a brief **Think-Pair-Share**, Book Talk, or piggyback into a Response Log as a writing activity. This discussion time can lead other students into wanting to read a book that their friend read. Remember to model how this time should look within your classroom! Pleasant reading experiences most likely instill a love of reading in your classroom. (See **WALKING THE WALK & TALKING THE TALK**.)

READ, HIDE & SEEK, THINK & SAY

From Linda Hoyt's *Revisit, Reflect, Retell: Strategies for Improving Reading Comprehension* (1999) comes our adapted version of her Read-Cover-Remember-Retell reading comprehension strategy from Jan Ellison.

The underlying purposes of Read, Hide & Seek, Think & Say are for readers of all ages to slow their reading rate down in order to increase reading comprehension. Unfortunately, many readers fail to stop periodically to check for understanding.

As with all of the other strategies included herein, you will need to model this strategy many times for your students. It works best when your students are asked to try it independently, or that they initially work with a partner who is reading the same book.

Many struggling students believe that as long as they are reading, they comprehend, and this just is not the case.

READ

Students select a small amount of passage to **Read**. This should be equivalent to an amount that they can cover with their hand, in a horizontal fashion. As they become better comprehenders, they can turn their hand vertically to cover more text.

HIDE & SEEK

After they have read the designated amount from the passage, they **Hide** the text with their hand. Students now **Seek** to recall what it is that they just read without looking back at the text. This is done quietly, setting the stage for the next step in the strategy. If they have trouble recollecting, this is what they do: they simply take a quick peek at the pictures, and/or reread the material.

THINK & SAY

The final phase of the strategy has the student **Think & Say** what they just read to their partner. This extra step of saying what they remember to a partner practices higher-order thinking because students are asked to explain their reading.

A final note: For middle and high school students, the length of the passage might be a column, page, or chapter in length. We would expect these students to incorporate many good reader strategies like **SQ3R**, or **E.I.P.** as they are reading.

JUST TWO

Just Two is an adaptation of Linda Hoyt's (1999) Two Word Strategy, from *Revisit, Reflect, Retell: Strategies for Improving Reading Comprehension*. It is a reading strategy that helps students reflect on what they have just read. Students are asked to remember important facts, details, and personal connections to the text they just read. Trying to recall everything is not only hard for all of us but also extremely frustrating for reluctant or struggling readers.

Students are given a small post-it note. Its size alone already calms many readers because they know that they will not have to write a paragraph or fill out a worksheet on what they just read.

❖ Select a short read-aloud book.

❖ Explain the strategy to the students. Tell them that they will be writing Just Two important words on a post-it note after you have finished reading the book. If you do not say just two, they will want to write more.

❖ These words must be important enough so that every time they think of these two words, it will remind them of the book. At first, some students will just copy the title onto their post-it note. With practice and continued modeling, the choice of words will change from title words to text-to-self or world connections.

❖ After you have read the book, give students time to think about the two words as you pass out the post-it notes. If you pass them out before you read, they will write the words during the story and not wait until the end. Tell them to write just two words, spelling does not count.

❖ The next step is for students to turn to their partner and share the reasons why they picked each word. This step is extremely crucial to learning. Sharing why they picked the words will help students connect with the words they chose.

❖ When all students have finished sharing, go around the room and ask each person to give you their favorite word or their partner's.

Just Two also works with content area reading. When reading a unit in social studies or science, students synthesize their reading into just two words. If you wanted to extend this activity even further, you could collect the post-it notes and add them to a **Word Mania** grid already started on this topic. While working on setting, characters, or main idea, students can write the names of two characters, two key ideas, or two details about the setting.

Example: Wendell reads *The Jolly Christmas Postman* by Janet Ahlberg and Allen Ahlberg. His two words are *sister* and *Iowa*. He chose *sister* because his sister, Wendy, is a postal carrier. He picked *Iowa* because she still resides in Cedar Falls, where his family was raised.

E.I.P.

Extremely Important Points or (E.I.P.) is an adaptation of Linda Hoyt's (1999) V.I.P. Strategy, from *Revisit, Reflect, Retell: Strategies for Improving Reading Comprehension*. E.I.P. is not just for overloaded readers but for everyone else too. The goal of E.I.P. is to remember the most important facts about a reading. When we read, we try to remember everything that we are reading. In some cases, when it comes to content area reading, this can be very frustrating. Chapters or sections are long and loaded with dates, people, ideas, and events!!!!

Students are given a post-it note that has been cut into 5 or 6 equal pieces, up to the sticky side. With primary students, you would use less strips and shorter texts. With older students and longer texts, you will need to adjust accordingly.

Model this strategy with a one page story or informational piece of reading on the overhead. As you are reading out loud, take a sticky note and begin marking the points that you find significant. If you run out of sticky notes before you have finished reading, you will have to weigh the importance of what you have already marked and move a sticky note. By modeling this process, students will see that when we read we are thinking about what we are reading. After you have finished reading, tell the students why you picked each Extremely Important Point and open it up for discussion. Giving reasons why the points were picked requires a higher-level of thinking.

Another variation of this activity is to pair students up and have them each mark the E.I.P.'s on the same passage. They can then discuss why they marked each point and come up with five points that they both agree on. Here again, we are encouraging the interactive environment that will have students engaging with text.

These Extremely Important Points transfer nicely into a summary. Not only is this easier to assess but it saves time and endless writing. Some students when asked for a summary can go on and on. E.I.P. teaches them how to be selective about the points they pick, because they have so few notes to mark. Adding an extra step of explaining these points to a partner will help build the higher-level thinking that we are so encouraging in our book.

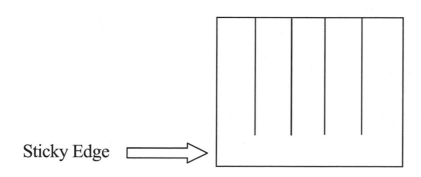

Sticky Edge

HIGHLIGHT THE BEST

Highlight the Best is a reading strategy that helps students determine what is important about what they are reading. If highlighters are not available, underlining will also work.

Highlight the Best helps to move novice reading towards critical reading by realizing that there are inferential clues that support the content being read. It helps students remember the topic and mark details that elaborate that topic into main ideas and conclusions.

Using photocopied or student-owned material, the student highlights only key words and phrases that deal with the topic or main idea. The final product will only have the words and phrases that are key to comprehending the author's intended purpose, thus eliminating extraneous or loosely related information that could confuse the reader.

STEPS FOR TEACHING HIGHLIGHT THE BEST

1. Reading material should be photocopied or student-owned.

2. Read the text out loud in its entirety.

3. Model the highlighting of single words or phrases, and content-heavy words, NOT whole sentences. Nouns are usually the most powerful words that can be highlighted because of the weight they carry.

4. Identify definitions and mark only significant details.

5. Discuss all the information that was highlighted and why it was marked.

6. Students will begin to notice that articles, conjunctions, and prepositions are insignificant words and do not need to be highlighted.

Make copies and distribute Highlight the Best Bookmarks located after **In the Margin**. Students should keep this bookmark handy and refer to it until they are able to do the strategy on their own.

Highlight the Best must be modeled at least five to ten times before the student can internalize the skill and it becomes a useful strategy. (See **MAKING CONNECTIONS**.)

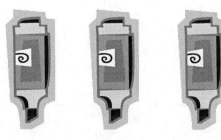

IN THE MARGIN

Like **Highlight the Best**, In the Margin allows the student to interact with the text, with the added feature of being able to respond to what is being read. In the Margin requires the student to pause and comment on the text in the margin, paragraph by paragraph. By jotting down questions, summarizing ideas, and writing key words, phrases or sketches every so often, the reader will be monitoring their own comprehension every step of the way.

Students can take notes on an order of events or steps in a procedure, if the text calls for it. They can clarify meaning whenever they come across a question or have a doubt.

One of the goals of In the Margin is to get students to *think* while they are reading and engage with the text in a meaningful way. (See **MAKING CONNECTIONS**.)

STEPS FOR TEACHING IN THE MARGIN

1. Reading material should be photocopied or student-owned.

2. Use material that has already been read once by the students.

3. The use of Highlight the Best information enhances this activity even further.

4. Model the strategy out loud using the overhead. Stop at the end of each paragraph and write a phrase, definition, sketch, or key word in the margin.

5. Draw a picture, symbol, or graphic organizer in the margin so students see that the text can sometimes ask the reader to make a mental picture.

6. Finish this activity by discussing all the marginal notations and why they were selected.

Make copies and distribute In the Margin Bookmarks located on the next page. Students should keep this bookmark handy and refer to it until they are able do the strategy on their own.

The "marked up" or "highlighted" text allows the student a level of INTERACTIVITY with what is being read. When students are able to interact with what they are reading, they are more apt to internalize the content and make it part of their prior knowledge. Simply reading material and doing nothing with it will show students that reading is just looking at words.

HIGHLIGHT THE BEST AND IN THE MARGIN BOOKMARKS

HIGHLIGHT OR UNDERLINE THE BEST

Highlighting/Underlining helps you search for details and examples that support the topic or main idea.

DO mark:
- ❖ definitions
- ❖ nouns (persons, places, things, or ideas)
- ❖ words and phrases (not whole sentences)
- ❖ supporting evidence
- ❖ at least one detail in each paragraph

Highlighting/Underlining does not replace comprehension.

Don't mark:
- ❖ topic more than once
- ❖ whole sentences
- ❖ numbers without context
- ❖ too much

What is highlighted or underlined represents the reader's JUDGMENT of details that carry SIGNIFICANCE in the text.

Remember, good readers:
- ❖ *Look for relationships*
- ❖ *Build complex knowledge*
- ❖ *Persist and re-read*

IN THE MARGIN

Marginal notes allow you to record your CONNECTIONS as you read text.

Make notes about:

- ❖ **Sequences:** *Is there an order of events?*

- ❖ **Questions:** *Are you unsure of the meaning of something?*

- ❖ **Drawings or Symbols:** *How can you represent this idea?*

- ❖ **Inferences:** *What is hinted at here?*

- ❖ **Implications:** *What could this lead to?*

- ❖ **Summarizing:** *What is the main idea?*

In the Margin allows you to TALK BACK to the text, paragraph by paragraph.

Remember, good readers:
- ❖ *Infer often*
- ❖ *Paraphrase ideas in their own words*
- ❖ *Monitor their understanding*

MAKING CONNECTIONS

Making Connections is a strategy that helps students categorize the information they are reading. By placing certain codes periodically throughout their reading, students are connecting with the material in some way. When first using this strategy, students should stop at the end of each paragraph and make some type of notation using the codes provided below. Later on, students can stop every few paragraphs or more.

The beauty of Making Connections is that students are able to comment on the text with questions, confusions, and acknowledgments. The nature of the codes allows them to use any of them when the need arises without feeling inferior because they do not understand certain sections of text.

This strategy should be modeled using text that may seem very unfamiliar to students. They will then be able to use as many of the codes as possible. Students can use small post-it notes to mark their codes onto their reading.

CODES

Question	**?**	**I have a question about this.**
Confusing	**C**	**I do not understand.**
Text to Self	**T-S**	**I understand what this is about.**
Text to Text	**T-T**	**I have read about this in another book.**
Text to World	**T-W**	**I have seen this in my surroundings.**
Background Knowledge	**BK**	**I know a lot about this subject.**
Personal Experience	**PE**	**I have had that happen to me.**

THINK-PAIR-SHARE

The use of Think-Pair-Share further enhances Making Connections. Just as the name suggests, this is a strategy to open up the channels of discussion with your students. It is pretty simple to implement, and takes virtually no preparation time. This activity is extremely powerful because every student is an active participant.

It can be used as a pre-reading strategy, a follow-up activity, or for problem solving. Students simply "Think" about the topic, "Pair" up with a partner, and "Share" their ideas about what they have just read or coded.

A follow-up might be to pull the class back together after partners have had the opportunity to share and lead a class discussion. Another activity that might be spawned from Think-Pair-Share would be for students to keep notes in their Writer's Journals, which, in turn, could branch off into a **Piggybacking** topic.

KEYS TO VOCABULARY BUILDING

A rich vocabulary allows a reader/writer to get a flavor or richness of thought. The real pleasure, however, comes from knowing and recognizing powerful vocabulary words and being able to use the right words in writing. Simply copying words and defining them will not help students remember words. Vocabulary is necessary not only for reading but for enhancing writing. Explicit instruction of vocabulary words is one of the keys to vocabulary building.

Vocabulary instruction is necessary for fluency reading because simply skipping the "big" words does not promote reading comprehension; in fact it hinders it tremendously. As teachers, we should select the "right" vocabulary words. Just because a text recommends which words we should use, does not mean that we cannot use some and select others. We want to select words that are important to remember for further reading and writing on the same topic.

Pre-teaching vocabulary words is another key to quality vocabulary instruction. When students learn the vocabulary words before they start reading, they will be able to engage with the text. We want students to make the important text-to-text, text-to-self, and text-to-world connections as they are reading instead of hitting a brick wall and spending valuable time trying to decode the words and not remember what they read.

Donavan's Word Jar by Monalisa Degross is an excellent read-aloud. Donavan is a third grade boy who collects words that sound funny, slide on his tongue, or make him feel different when he sees them. You will just have to read the book to find out what happens to Donavan's word jar. Keeping a word jar in your classroom will let the students bring in words they think are important to remember.

Another key to vocabulary building is to practice the words in a variety of ways and contexts. Variety is the key, because we have so many learning styles in our classrooms! Students should also be able to practice vocabulary words in centers. Centers help you to individualize learning. The more students can practice the vocabulary words, the more they will be able to read these words fluently when faced with them in context and use them while writing.

Vocabulary mapping, (on the next page), helps the struggling learner see that words have many parts to them. A graphic organizer of a new vocabulary word can have synonyms, parts of speech, a definition, and even a picture.

The last key to vocabulary building is reading! Students should have plenty of opportunities to independently read material at their interest and ability level. Yes, the more you read, the better you get. Not only does this enrich your background knowledge, but it also provides the struggling reader *with* the comfort level of reading material that will help with fluency and comprehension. (See **INSTILLING THE LOVE OF READING**.)

Vocabulary words are not spelling words! These words do not go on your Word Wall. Word Wall Words are high frequency words that you want your students to spell correctly all the time. How often do you use and spell the word photosynthesis? (See **LIANNE'S LANGUAGE LINK**.)

VOCABULARY MAPPING

Vocabulary Mapping—This strategy will aid students in expanding their vocabulary development using a simple mapping format.

1. The students place the vocabulary word in the middle of a blank piece of paper.

2. They label each of the four corners of the paper with the following headings; definition, synonym, sentence, and picture.

3. Then, students draw arrows radiating from the vocabulary word to each of the four headings.

4. Next, students complete what is being asked for under each of the four headings in regards to the vocabulary word.

5. Finally, students share and discuss their vocabulary mappings with each other or as a class.

    ❖ The visual appeal of this graphic organizer will help reach your visual/spatial learners.

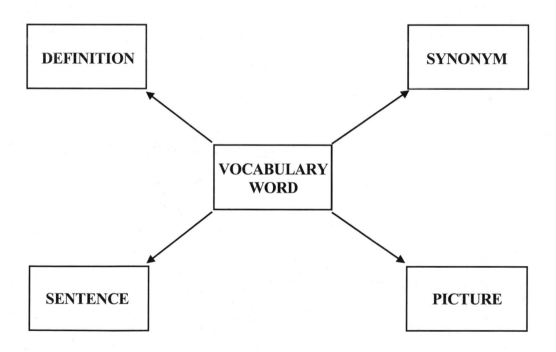

    ❖ **EXTENSION**: These words can be cut out and added to other vocabulary words for a match-up game and placed in a center for further practice.

Q.A.R.

How often have you sat up late at night correcting papers and wondered why students keep getting a question wrong when the answer is right there? Well, one of the most powerful strategies you will find in our book is right here! This strategy is not only good for elementary students as low as second grade, but high school and beyond.

This strategy is so amazing that just modeling it a few times will have your students identifying which type of question you are asking! Raphael developed Q.A.R. or Question Answer Relationship in 1982. Its main purpose is to teach students how questions are formulated, thus enabling the students to find the answers much quicker. Questions move from literal to inferential on a comprehension continuum. Once this strategy has been modeled, students can begin to make up their own questions.

What are these types of questions?

❖ **Right There** questions are those questions for which students will find the answer in one sentence of the text, using some of the exact words found in the question. Students are not allowed to get these questions wrong because the answers are right there! Duh! We have taught our students this phrase because it is the feeling we get when we know that the answer is right there!

❖ **Here and There** questions are those questions for which students will find the answer in several places of the text. Part of the answer may be in one paragraph or sentence and the other part may be somewhere else in the text. Students will need to use the question's key words or synonyms to help them locate the answer.

❖ **You and Me** questions are those questions where the students will have to read what the author has written and use their own prior knowledge to answer the question. This type of question involves a higher-level of thinking. Students will use synonyms or key words from the text to stimulate their prior knowledge and help them answer the question.

❖ **Just Me** types of questions involve the students answering the question on their own. The student can answer this question without even reading the text by using key words from the question.

Using a relatively short passage with already prepared questions, (trust us, they are everywhere) model this strategy on the overhead. By highlighting the key words in the question and showing students where in the passage the exact answers are, you are modeling for students that questions are not always as difficult as they believe to answer.

This strategy is one of the most **important** reading comprehension strategies you will find in our book or anywhere else for that matter. By teaching Q.A.R. to all of your students, you are empowering them with the ability to get many questions right on standardized testing or any other test. What a feeling!

STEPS FOR Q.A.R.

1. Students will identify key words, usually nouns, or verbs by highlighting or circling them. Remind them to pay close attention to the punctuation also. Step 1 is the most important step!

2. Students then try to find the same key words in the text that are in the question.

3. Now, students will look at the remaining words in that sentence for the answer to the question. This type of response is literally **Right There**. (Duh!)

   Did they find the answer after step 3? If they did not, they will continue to step 4.

4. Have students continue to look for the question's key words in the text or synonyms for them. This step will require them to look in more than one sentence for the answer to the question. Be careful! Some students will stop when they find part of the answer and not want to continue searching.

5. They will connect the information from the sentences where they found the key words or synonyms to synthesize their answer. This type of response is called **Here and There**.

   Did they find the answer after steps 4 and 5? If they did not, they will continue to step 6.

6. The use of the author's clues and their prior knowledge will assist students in this step. They should look for the question's key words, synonyms, or concepts throughout the text.

7. This information should stimulate their prior knowledge to answer the question. This type of question is known as **You and Me**.

   If they still have not found the answer in the text, they should continue on.

8. By now students must be wondering if they did something wrong. Not necessarily! In this final step of the comprehension continuum, their answer will be found in their own prior knowledge.

9. Students will use the key words, concepts, or ideas in the question to stimulate their own prior knowledge in order to answer the question. This is a self-actualizing type response, inferential in nature, and known as **Just Me**.

Q.A.R. is especially powerful in middle and high school where students are exposed to many questions in a long unit or chapter.

GUIDELINES FOR ASKING QUESTIONS

Curiosity won't kill the cat! Questions are the key to understanding. Questions will propel the students into a higher-level of thinking and allow them to make sense of the world around them. Asking effective questions is the key to extending comprehension. Carefully prepared questions will do this as long as the questions are not strictly at the recall level. (See **RECIPROCAL TEACHING, MAKING CONNECTIONS & KWL**.)

Model these before-reading activities: view the cover, read the title, flip through the pages, make text-to-self (T-S), text-to-text (T-T), or text-to-world (T-W) predictions. Generate questions about the topic or concept. Students should ask themselves speculative and predictive questions. You will be encouraging students to ask their own questions when it is their turn to engage in the task on their own. Students who practice these strategies, and frequently ask themselves questions, will soon become independent learners and comprehenders.

Some questions students might ask themselves are:

- ❖ What do I already know about the topic or concept?
- ❖ Is this like anything else I have studied?
- ❖ I already know this, but do not know about….
- ❖ What would I like to learn from this passage or text?

TEACHER'S ROLE IN THIS PROCESS

After you have read about the topic or concept, model the following self-questioning techniques:

- ❖ Ask questions on the high end of the questioning scale. (Analysis, Synthesis, & Evaluation)
- ❖ Ask a minimum number of questions that rely only on recall.
- ❖ What writing elements made me think or feel a certain way?
- ❖ Was I able to answer my questions? If not, why not?

When used correctly, students are required to answer literal and inferential types of questions. They will ask themselves these types of questions throughout a passage or text. This information processing and self-monitoring technique will dramatically increase comprehension.

WAIT! Yes, after asking a question, pause (Wait Time). This brief moment of silence allows the student to process the question and formulate a response. The amount of "Wait Time" is dependent on the complexity of the question, according to **Bloom's Taxonomy**. Five to ten seconds should be an adequate amount of time to wait.

BLOOM'S TAXONOMY OF HIGHER LEVEL QUESTIONING

❖ **KNOWLEDGE:** checks for <u>basic</u> facts about people, places, or things.
Key words = who, what, where, when, how, describe, define, choose, and select.

1. When does the story take place?
2. Where did _____ live?
3. Who is the main character in the story?

❖ **COMPREHENSION:** checks understanding and memory.
Key words = give an example, explain, summarize, demonstrate, infer, show, classify, facts/opinions, and condense.

1. Describe what happened after _____.
2. Explain how _____ arrived at _____.
3. How were _____ and _____ related?

❖ **APPLICATION:** ability to use your knowledge of facts, rules, and principles.
Key words = predict, identify results of, judge the effects of, tell how, when, where and why, and tell what would happen if.

1. How would you feel if_____?
2. Predict what will happen next.
3. Do you think _____?

❖ **ANALYSIS:** break into smaller parts.
Key words = distinguish, conclusions, identify, theme, main idea, relationship between, and point of view.

1. Compare _____ to _____.
2. Analyze how _____ lived or acted.
3. Which event was most exciting? Why?

❖ **SYNTHESIS:** use basic information and combine it to create a new pattern or whole.
Key words = create, compose, develop, propose an alternative, how else would you, do, make, and design.

1. Which character in the story would you like to be? Why?
2. How would this story be different if it were to take place in another country?
3. Create a different ending for this story or event.

❖ **EVALUATION:** help you decide the value of the information gained.
Key words = appraise, judge, criticize, defend, compare, and find the errors.

1. Predict what will happen next.
2. Recreate an event in the story using animals instead of people.
3. What is your opinion of _____?

ACCORDING TO THE CUBE

According to the Cube will have students orally responding to one of six reading comprehension strategies. It is designed for students to rapidly consider their subject from six points of view: knowledge (recall), comprehension, application, analysis, synthesis, and evaluation.

Preparation on the teacher's part is to construct a cube with each of **Bloom's Taxonomy** words attached to one face of the cube. An easy way to do this would be to purchase oversized dice and use a label for attaching the words.

This is a perfect activity for cooperative groups. After the cube is rolled and a level is displayed, students discuss that strategy of comprehension within their group. Before, during, and after reading about a subject, students discuss their perspective until the teacher calls time. Approximately three to five minutes discussion time should be allowed before rolling the cube again, using the same reading subject, but answering different questions from a different perspective. Repeat two to three times before proceeding. Adjust time according to the level of your students. More time for discussion might be needed at the middle and high school level.

According to the Cube will offer the teacher vehicles for discussions, stimulate sharing and oral discussions of ideas, and act as a post-reading activity, or a means to review before a test.

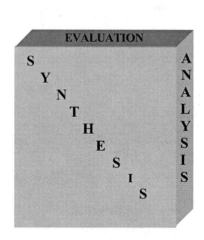
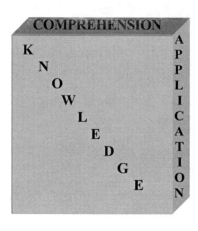

Adapted from:
Vaughn, J. L. & Estes, T.H. (1986). *Reading and Reasoning Beyond the Primary Grades.* Boston: Allyn & Bacon, Inc.

SQ3R

SQ3R is another reading comprehension strategy that your students can easily assimilate into their quiver of learned strategies. Each step of the SQ3R strategy should be introduced, modeled, and explained in detail so students know how to perform the task. Provide guided practice as each step is introduced for maximum student ownership.

As you begin, you may notice that many other strategies within this book seem similar and somewhat overlapping. There is no need to be alarmed by this fact. Your students will see the similarities and understand that often one strategy is more effective than another, depending upon the lesson objective.

S = Survey. This is another term for previewing text. Ask your students to survey the text, reading heading and sub headings, bold face words, and glance at any pictures. The part of SQ3R that is different from other strategies is that it specifically asks readers to scan the chapter summary. Surveying the chapter and reading the chapter summary will give students an idea of the main points. Questions that students can ask themselves might include: "What will the chapter be about?" or "What do I already know?" The value of this technique is to help students focus on the main points of each chapter.

Q = Question. Demonstrate how to convert chapter headings into questions. The value of questioning is that it arouses curiosity and sets a purpose for reading. This activity leads directly into outlining. Show your students the correlation between this activity and **Power Notes.**

R = Read. Students begin to read the text looking for the answers to their questions. During this segment, students should put into practice their learned comprehension monitoring strategies (stopping to understand, identifying key concepts, and vocabulary, etc…). If they are unable to answer their questions, a rereading of the passage may be necessary. During this rereading, students may want to use **Highlight the Best** for additional emphasis on focusing attention to answering their questions.

R = Recite. Students should flip back through the pages and reflect on what has been read. Have them think about the answers to their questions, recite them orally, or jot them down on paper. Ask questions like: "What information was important?" "What judgments can be made about prioritizing information?" "How were you able to get the answers to your questions?" "If you were unsuccessful, what could be done differently?"

R = Review. Ask students what connections can be made between the information they read and what they already knew. Begin this step by reviewing headings, subheadings, etc… just like in surveying the text. Students should be able to recall the main points of the passage. A final step would be for the students to write a brief summary.

Adapted from:
Johns, J.L. & Lenski, S. D. (1997) *Improving Reading: A Handbook of Strategies* (2nd ed). Iowa: Kendall/Hunt

SQ3R GUIDE

SURVEY: (Clues from the title, headings, pictures, etc...)

The text, chapter, passage, or story will be about:

QUESTIONS: (Students formulate questions based upon headings, including the use of who, what, when, where, why, and how questions.)

1.

2.

3.

4.

READ: (Students use good reader strategies throughout the text, by coding important information and listing any points that surprise or really interest them.)

RECITE: (These are the answers to the questions that were generated. Students should use memory techniques to recall what they have just learned.)

1.

2.

3.

4.

REVIEW: (Students review the text in the same fashion as in surveying the text. Have students try to recall as many main points as they can without looking back into the text.)

Adapted from:
Johns, J.L. & Lenski, S. D. (1997) *Improving Reading: A Handbook of Strategies* (2nd ed). Iowa: Kendall/Hunt

POWER NOTES

Power Notes is just another way of outlining information from a text, or it can be used as a means of organizing ideas before writing. It is designed to help students differentiate between main ideas and details. The main ideas will be assigned Power 1's, and details will be assigned Power 2's, 3's and so on. (See **WORD SORTING & E.I.P.**)

Students will need to be introduced to the following scaffolding chart in order to grasp the concept. Display this on the board or overhead for students to use as a reference.

Power 1: Main Idea
    Power 2: Detail and support for power 1
        Power 3: Detail and support for power 2
            Power 4: Detail and support for power 3

An easy way to introduce the idea of using Power Notes is by using words instead of text. An example might be as follows:

Power 1: States
    Power 2: Midwestern States
        Power 3: Iowa
        Power 3: Minnesota
            Power 4: Land of 10,000 Lakes
    Power 2: Southeastern States
        Power 3: Florida
        Power 3: Georgia

To further practice with the students, have them pick a topic such as television, video games, sports, or food. When students have a firm understanding, extend this activity by assigning topics and having the students complete the activity in cooperative groups.

The use of Power Notes structures students in their thinking before they develop their writing. How easy it will be for students to simply follow the outline to develop their main ideas! These simple paragraphs are the foundation in which students will build longer writing assignments.

Keep in mind that the overuse of any formula can hinder creativity and slow the progress of those students who have already internalized a sense of structure. Be careful and monitor each student individually.

For use with text, simply select something that students can work on at their independent level. Using **Highlight the Best**, have students organize the information by powers. Remember to start with text that is fairly short in length. As students gain confidence, the text can be longer and from content areas. (See **HIGHLIGHT THE BEST**.)

POWER NOTES MATRIX

Use this matrix to assist students in outlining information. This form may be copied for the students and made into an overhead transparency for an easy teaching tool. Remember that Power Notes are designed to differentiate between main ideas and details. The example immediately below is only the basic framework to Power Notes. You may have more than one Power 2, 3, or 4.

Power 1: Main Idea (topic idea)
    Power 2: Detail and support for Power 1
        Power 3: Detail and support for Power 2
            Power 4: Detail and support for Power 3

Use the following empty chart to assist your students as they learn how to develop Power Notes or create one with similar structure.

Power 1: _____

    Power 2: _____

    Power 2: _____

        Power 3: _____

        Power 3: _____

            Power 4: _____

    Power 2: _____

    Power 2: _____

        Power 3: _____

        Power 3: _____

            Power 4: _____

            Power 4: _____

You will find a variation of Power Notes in the Graphic Organizer section that may be easier for students in primary grades to use. Middle and high school students should be successful using the one above since it is really just outlining.

RECIPROCAL TEACHING

Annemarie Sullivan Palincsar and Ann L. Brown developed this extremely powerful comprehension strategy. Reciprocal Teaching encourages the development of skills that are used by strategic readers. The strategy allows students to use four specific strategies (predicting, clarifying, questioning, and summarizing) to resolve their problems in their comprehension. Research tells us that it takes twenty lessons of explicit instruction before students can successfully do Reciprocal Teaching on their own.

In order for students to take ownership of Reciprocal Teaching, the teacher must model it repeatedly so students understand the interactive, supportive, and accountable format in which discussion takes place. After this, the teacher will then act as a coach (leader) sitting in with a group of students to monitor student discussions. Later, as the students become more confident in their understanding of the strategy, it transitions from teacher-directed instruction to a more cooperative learning environment. This consistent structure sets the objective of the lesson, and students will be more successful.

In our adaptation of Reciprocal Teaching, students will gradually assume the teacher's role as leader. This new leader will use the set of Leader Cards to facilitate the discussion and examination of the text. The Leader Cards are used not only to test recall and comprehension, but they are also designed to have students thinking at the application, analysis, and synthesis levels of **Bloom's Taxonomy**. The teacher will then act as a classroom monitor helping groups of students needing guided instruction.

The materials that can be used for Reciprocal Teaching are endless. Many teachers use articles, content specific texts, stories, newspapers, and magazines. A note of caution: Begin with easy readability, and relatively short texts. We want to build upon success, not overwhelm them with too much material. The skills included in Reciprocal Teaching will transfer directly into independent reading.

You will find the Leader Cards for Reciprocal Teaching on the next two pages.

RECIPROCAL TEACHING LEADER CARDS

Card 1

"Please get ready to read to _____ in our material."

- ❖ *Remember to preview the text, look for boldface words, and glance at pictures.*
- ❖ *Choose a natural stopping point in the text.*

Card 2

"I predict that this section of text will be about _____."

- ❖ *As leader, offer a prediction of the text.*
- ❖ *Think about who, what, when, where, why, and how predictions.*
- ❖ *This prediction should be based upon the previewing strategies mentioned in Card 1.*

Card 3

"What other predictions might we be able to make?"

- ❖ *The leader encourages other group members for their ideas and predictions.*

Card 4

"We will now read the text together out loud. "

- ❖ *Primary should read out loud, intermediate should whisper read, and middle and high school should whisper or silent read.*
- ❖ *Read only to the designated stopping point chosen in Card 1.*

RECIPROCAL TEACHING LEADER CARDS

Card 5

"Are there any words or concepts that you thought were interesting or had questions about?"

❖ *Do not say, "Are there any words you did not understand?"*
❖ *As leader, you are responsible for clarifying any misconceptions.*

Card 6

"Any I wonder questions? What did you find interesting and why?"

❖ *Is clarification needed for any parts of the text?*
❖ *This type of answer calls for a more sophisticated response.*

Card 7

"This section of the reading was about _____."

❖ *As leader, summarize the material in one or two sentences.*

Card 8

"Does any group member wish to add to the summary?"

❖ *Allow group members to add information to the summary, if needed.*

THE CATEGORY IS?

After children become familiar with **Power Notes** and **Word Sorting**, this interactive activity will further their understanding of Main Ideas.

This activity uses 3 x 5 index cards with a word or picture placed upon each card. You **do not** label (Power 1's etc…) or describe the categories prior to their exploration. It will be the role of the students to decide how the things are alike.

To begin with, students will cluster two or three pictures that have similarities together. An example might be zoo animals, foods, or green objects. They will continue to sort the cards until all cards have been placed into groups where they believe they belong. Next, the students will come up with the name of their categories (main ideas).

The Category Is items can be placed in centers or stations around the room. Emergent to beginning readers can dictate or discuss the category with a teacher assistant, parent volunteer, or older buddy reader. This activity can also be done in cooperative groups. To extend this activity for older students, have them use index cards to create more sorts or categories of their own.

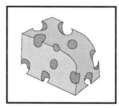

FUNCTIONAL READING

Functional Reading is material that is typically encountered in everyday life. We read directions on how to make a cake from the back of the box. We decide if we want to buy something based on a newspaper advertisement. Trying to be health conscious, we look at the ingredients of our favorite snack food. These are all examples of functional reading. Our students need to be exposed to this everyday reading material too. One of the easiest ways to do this is through cereal and snack boxes. Once you get the ball rolling, your students will be bringing in their favorite boxes to share.

Using all the sides of a cereal box, come up with questions that will address a list of ingredients, how much it would cost to order the item being sold on the back (here is some math), how many servings are in the box, etc. Your students can practice the steps it takes to make cupcakes and what would happen if they substituted one ingredient for another. Students will begin to think about their everyday life and how reading is a part of everything they do.

The Sunday newspaper has many inserts with coupons, recipes and the ordering of items from coffee cups to figurines. Because they are in color, all you have to do is cut them out, glue them to construction paper, and laminate them. By writing the questions on the bottom of the card, you can write the answers on the back. Students love to do this because it is easy, quick, and fun. Having the answers on the back, makes this a great center activity. It is self-checking, provides immediate feedback and you do not have to take a bag of papers home.

Restaurant menus are also a fun way to practice Functional Reading. Most restaurants have take-out menus. Laminate these and write a few questions where students are asked to carefully scrutinize some of the items on the menu. Have them write out what they would order if they were to go there with a certain amount of money. Now you are not only teaching them how to order from a menu but they are also practicing math skills.

WHAT IS A MINI PAGE?

A Mini Page is one whole page of your local newspaper that is devoted to children and families. Betty Debnam publishes it once a week, all over the country. Mainly targeted to children, the Mini Page offers a variety of topics written at children's readability levels. Each week the Mini Page focuses on a different topic from historical to current events. It has sections on cooking easy recipes **(Functional Reading)**, word searches, and famous people in history. Students of all ages enjoy doing the Mini Page because it offers short bits of information that do not overwhelm the struggling reader and challenge and entertain the good reader.

Cut out the sections of the mini page, glue them onto a file folder and laminate it for longevity. Besides enjoying these Mini Pages for their content, we would like to offer a few more uses. Have students circle the high frequency words using a Vis-à-vis pen. If you are working on a particular grammar skill, have students locate them also. Another fun activity is to look for little words within big words.

This is a great center activity. For more information, go to www.minipage.com. You will be able to find additional teacher resources and information.

A PENNY FOR YOUR THOUGHTS!

A Penny for Your Thoughts was adapted from Roger Farr's, "What are you thinking?" This strategy is so much fun that you will want to start it as soon as you return to your classroom. As we have mentioned over and over again in our book, one of our goals is to get students to think more when they are reading and writing. A Penny for Your Thoughts will do just that. Basically, all you are doing is getting your students to periodically stop every so often and tell you what they are thinking.

Using social studies or science text, begin by reading a portion of it out loud and stop at the end of a paragraph. Then say, "A Penny for Your Thoughts!" The student that gives you a fact or statement about what you just read gets a paper penny. At the beginning of this activity, your students will probably answer, nothing. As they start to think more about their reading, and the strategies throughout this book are practiced, you will see that they really do have plenty to say. We just are not used to letting them talk because we are doing all the talking. Students can collect these paper pennies. After some time, you can vary this activity by taking away pennies when they do not give you the information you ask for.

Once your students have a firm hold on this strategy, you can circulate around the room during independent reading, or content area reading. Stop by a few students and say, "A Penny for Your Thoughts!" Since students will never know when you are going to do this, they will want to be ready for you. Guess who won? We did! They are thinking while reading and we have accomplished one of the most major goals of our teaching career: To produce independent learners!

JEOPARDY

This activity will have your students looking in newspapers, magazines, and content area textbooks to come up with new categories for the game. Yes, they will probably even watch television at night to pick up additional categories, strategies to win, and bring to school topics to discuss and learn.

The teacher should be the moderator or game host until students understand how the game is played. A pocket chart works well to hold and display the answers. Remember, the students will have to come up with the questions!

Prepare value cards like that on the game show (100-500). Remember to place a "Double Jeopardy" card somewhere so it cannot be seen. These should be displayed first, covering up the answer card. We use a pocket chart for this activity. On one side of a 4 x 6 index card, you will display the answer about a particular category. On the opposing side of that same card, the question is given. By using this process, students will be able to work cooperatively in pairs or groups of three's to play the game.

The game can be won be adding up point value cards, or by keeping track of how many each student got correct. Do not allow too much time to elapse for a correct question in response to the answer. It facilitates itself best when the tempo is quick!

For younger students, pictures work best and the teacher will need to moderate. A picture of an elephant on one side, and on the other the written form "elephant." Middle and high school students could create answers and questions for content area categories.

The moderator's role: read the clue (answer).
Player's role: respond by phrasing the response in the form of a question.

JEOPARDY

MOVIES	DATES	"ING" WORDS	STUFF	COMICS	SIMILES	LOGOS
100	100	100	100	100	100	100
200	200	200	200	200	200	200
300	300	300	300	300	300	300
400	400	400	400	400	400	400
500	500	500	500	500	500	500

CONCENTRATION

This game pairs student against student as each attempts to find word pairs or sets of related information. For the emergent learner, this might be in the form of pictures, and for those students that have mastered reading, the game can be played with: words and their definitions, homophone pairs, synonym and antonym pairs, or word phrases. (See **ADDING SPICE TO WRITING**.)

The game is played by facing all cards face down on a flat playing surface, or simply insert the cards into a pocket chart. Players take turns turning over two cards at a time, looking for a match. If the two cards "match" the player continues on with an additional turn, until no matches are made. The winner is determined by whoever holds the most matches at the conclusion of the game.

Students then shuffle the cards and randomly place the cards out for another game. The kinesthetic and visual nature of this activity will engage even the most challenged learners.

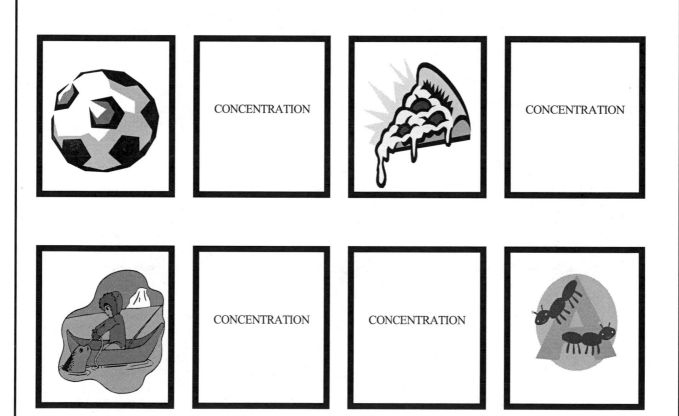

COMICS CUT TO SEQUENCE

Many of your students will gladly bring you in a steady supply of Sunday comics for this sequencing activity.

NOTE: Before you cut up the comics, pay careful attention to the order that they appear in the newspaper. The difficulty level of this activity will range from easy to complex, depending upon the comic.

After the comic strip is cut, simply glue or paste each segment onto a slightly oversized piece of construction paper. On the back of each segmented piece of comic, number them in the correct order as displayed in the newspaper. This step is done so students can self-check and self-correct. Laminate the materials for longevity and keep them clipped in a zip-lock baggy.

The comic strips should be placed in a pocket chart out of order for easy viewing and manipulating by the student.

Extensions for this activity can include: use comics written in a foreign language (more visual clues will be used), ask students to continue writing the comic strip, omit one segment and have them fill in the missing piece, or white out all of the speech bubbles and let the students write what they think each character's speech bubble might contain. Middle and high school students love these. At first glance, they think they are easy, but, upon trying them, they will not want to stop. (See **www.readingandwritingstrategically.com** for pictures)

SMARTY PANTS

This is a game for all of those "smarty pants" in your room that think they know all the answers. It is a game of everyday situations (really cause and effect).

After this has been modeled with the whole class, cooperative groups will facilitate better participation from all students.

The first player begins by giving an everyday situation in a simple way. For example:

"My dog escaped."

The next person must tell the reason why. For example:

"Because the trap door was left open."

The third person must figure out a probable effect. For example:

"And that is why the dog was caught by animal control."

The next player begins the process again with a simple description. The key is spontaneity, not whether or not the answer is the best. In a nutshell, a description is followed by a cause, then an effect. Enjoy!

CLOZE

The Cloze procedure, developed by Wilson L. Taylor (1953), is based upon the psychology theory of closure, which presumes that a person wishes to finish any incomplete pattern. The Cloze procedure is therefore based upon the prediction aspects of reading, which indicates that a reader wants to predict the unknown words in a passage. This procedure makes use of both semantic and syntactic cues to help a reader deduce the unknown words while reading.

When a text passage is prepared in Cloze format, some words are omitted. Spaces or lines are inserted to indicate where these words have been left out. The reader must use the meaning and structure of the remaining text to determine which word could be used to fill each space and restore meaning to the entire passage.

In standard Cloze format, every **n**th word is omitted in a regular pattern from a passage of continuous, meaningful text. Typically, every fifth, eighth, or eleventh word is left out. This format is used in Cloze materials written for testing purposes. In this format, only the exact word used in the original text is accepted as correct.

CLOZE PROCESS

The best way to begin the Cloze process with your students is by reading aloud. Select a fairly easy book and begin reading the book. Every few sentences pause and have the students predict what the missing word could be. By using their prior knowledge, picture clues, and content, they will begin to understand that reading is all about connecting thoughts and making mental pictures. Once students have grasped the concept, they are ready to try it on their own.

1. Select a passage and omit content words. Ask students to read the entire passage. This is a MUST!

2. Read the passage aloud modeling effective reading strategies.

3. As the passage is read, have students suggest words that might be written on the blank lines. If students have difficulty thinking of words to suggest, point out the clues that appear before and after each line, as well as the clues that occur elsewhere in the passage. Remember to look for picture clues, if they are available.

4. Have students give you reasons why they have chosen certain words. This encourages higher-level thinking.

❖ Reread the entire passage, substituting their word choices for the omitted words. Does the passage make sense now? If not, look back at the words they chose and change the ones that do not seem to fit. Now, reread the entire passage again to monitor understanding. Students should be able to complete each exercise with 75 percent accuracy.

❖ The Cloze process is an excellent activity to be used by students in a center for independent learning.

SUMMARIZING NARRATIVE READING

Summarizing Narrative Reading is a strategy to improve comprehension, develop an awareness of story structure, and increase vocabulary development.

Research shows that students' comprehension is enhanced when they are able to make some type of personal connection with what they are reading. Sensory perception words can help students accomplish this. Asking students to use at least one of their senses (tasting, touching, smelling, hearing, and seeing) to explain what they are reading not only enriches the task but also helps to form the much-needed connection.

Select a story. List vocabulary words that contain important concepts from the story. It is important to be able to recognize, pronounce, and have some understanding of the words.

Example: *Maniac Magee* by Jerry Spinelli

Maniac	Two Mills	Amanda	zoo	knot	baseball glove
backyard	railroad	school	East End	trolley	superhero

Using the story frame matrix, place the vocabulary words where students predict they belong.

NARRATIVE FRAME

SETTING	CHARACTERS	PROBLEM	SOLUTION	SENSORY PERCEPTION	ENDING

The main elements (setting, characters, problem, solution, and ending) for the Narrative Matrix will need to be filled in accordingly.

NARRATIVE MATRIX

The story takes place _____. (**SETTING**)

(**CHARACTER**) _____ is a character in the story.

In this story (**PROBLEM & SOLUTION**)_____
_____

The story ends (**ENDING**)_____

NARRATIVE FRAME

SETTING	CHARACTERS	PROBLEM	SOLUTION	SENSORY PERCEPTION	ENDING

NARRATIVE MATRIX

The story takes place _____. (SETTING)

(CHARACTER) _____ is a character in the story.

In this story (PROBLEM & SOLUTION) _____
_____
_____
_____
_____
_____

The story ends (ENDING)_____
_____
_____
_____
_____

SUMMARIZING EXPOSITORY READING

Summarizing Expository Reading is a strategy that helps students understand what they are reading when faced with expository text.

Research shows that students' comprehension is enhanced when they are able to make some type of personal connection with what they are reading. Sensory perception words can help students accomplish this. Asking students to use at least one of their senses (tasting, touching, smelling, hearing, and seeing) to explain what they are reading not only enriches the task but also helps to form the much-needed connection.

Using any type of expository text, such as a science book, select a chapter, or unit to read. List any relevant vocabulary or key terms found in that section. It is important that students be able to recognize and pronounce the key terms they are about to read.

The example below contains vocabulary words from a section of a science text. Place the vocabulary words where students predict they belong.

Forest Ecosystems

forest	deciduous	habitat	tropical	canopy	coastal
coniferous	plants	weather	animals	leaves	understory

EXPOSITORY FRAME

SETTING	CHARACTERISTICS DESCRIPTION	MAIN IDEA	CONNECTION	SENSORY PERCEPTION

EXPOSITORY MATRIX

(**SETTING**) The text/unit/chapter was about _____
_____

(**CHARACTERISTICS**) This section included specific descriptions of _____
_____

(**MAIN IDEA**) The key points were _____
_____

(**SUMMARY**) This section was about _____
_____

EXPOSITORY FRAME

SETTING	CHARACTERISTICS DESCRIPTION	MAIN IDEA	CONNECTION	SENSORY PERCEPTION

EXPOSITORY MATRIX

(SETTING) The text/unit/chapter was about _____
_____
_____
_____

(CHARACTERISTICS) This section included specific descriptions of _____
_____
_____
_____
_____

(MAIN IDEA) The key points were _____
_____
_____
_____

(SUMMARY) This section was about _____
_____
_____
_____

WALKING THE WALK & TALKING THE TALK

We have saved this page to the last in this section in our attempt to demonstrate how we have created a center for literacy learning. As we have said throughout *Reading and Writing Strategically*, strategies should be intertwined to maximize student learning and "raise the bar of expectations." Our students enjoy this center because they get to practice a variety of strategies. Without further ado, one of our centers:

READING CENTER

DIRECTIONS:

1. Students read the selected book or choose one on the topic of study. Remind them to use good reader strategies. Could they begin with the first step of **SQ3R**?

2. While reading, they practice the strategy **Read, Hide & Seek, Think & Say** by themselves, or with a partner.

3. After they are done reading the text, they complete the following:

   ❖ Independently, use the **Just Two** strategy. Write down two words on a Post-it-Note that reflect their understanding of the book. Share the selected words with a partner (**Think-Pair-Share**). They can discuss similarities and differences in the words they both chose.

   ❖ Have them select one word from the two words they wrote down on the Post-it-Note that they liked the best and have them write the word on the class **Word Mania Chart**. *(We are building vocabulary that will later be used in writing.)*

   ❖ Students can also practice, **A Penny for Your Thoughts!** with a partner at the reading center.

   ❖ Before they leave the Reading Center:

      i. Have them read the words on the Word Mania Chart.
      ii. Discuss the words chosen by other classmates with a partner.
      iii. Finally, they place their Post-it-Note beside the Word Mania Chart for accountability.

These strategies are designed to take reading comprehension beyond recall, and to a synthesized level of understanding. We counted at least seven strategies, including **Word Jar**, how many did you count?

EXTENSION: When a student comes across an extremely powerful vocabulary word, what should they do? It should be placed in the class **Word Jar**.

SECTION NOTES

FEEDBACK

TRAFFIC COURT

SECTION 4
WRITING STRATEGIES AND ACTIVITIES

PUBLISHING

I DON'T KNOW WHAT TO WRITE!

DOODLES-TO-DETAILS

WRITER'S WORKSHOP

The Writing Strategies and Activities section is designed for teachers who believe in process writing. Many in the educational field refer to this rationale of writing where the focus is the children, not the curriculum, "a community of learners" approach. This methodology has students accessing a variety of writing instruments: paper, pens, glue, construction paper, magazines, books, and markers or crayons that they can use while building their writing projects.

In this type of writing environment, students pull ideas from Writer's Journals, **"I Don't Know What to Write"** topics, **Piggybacking** samples, something new, or pulled from a writing folder where students keep all writing assignments. Students could possibly have a **Doodles-to-Details** activity started that relates to the project they are working on stored in their folder also.

Writer's Workshop is an established, daily, set time within a classroom set aside solely for the purpose of allowing students to write and publish their compositions. In the example below we have scheduled forty-five, uninterrupted minutes. The schedule includes time for a focused Mini-Lesson (5-10 minutes), where the teacher models a specific skill or strategy. Independent Practice (20-30 minutes) is time set aside for students to practice and apply the strategy. Finally, there should be sharing, (5-10 minutes) where students might even sit in an author's chair receiving guidance and feedback from their peers.

Take special notice that Writer's Workshop does not start with prewriting on Monday, drafting on Tuesday, revising on Wednesday, editing on Thursday, and sharing on Friday. It is just far too difficult to determine how long a piece of writing will take a student. In our classrooms, we expect students, with very few exceptions, to publish a writing piece about every two weeks, give or take a couple of days.

WRITING BLOCK

SHARING

MINI LESSON

INDEPENDENT PRACTICE

I DON'T KNOW WHAT TO WRITE!

This activity commonly referred by Peter Elbow as Free Writes and Gail Tompkins as Quickwriting now has a new name. I Don't Know What To Write, as the name suggests, is frequently heard throughout many classrooms. It is commonly known as "blank-page syndrome" or an inability to start writing. Often students "freeze" when they look at a clean, blank piece of writing paper, or erase sentence after sentence in their attempt to create a masterpiece with an exciting lead that grabs the reader's attention. I Don't Know What To Write lends itself to lowering anxiety levels within students as they begin to write imperfectly, with confidence, after initially starting with two or three sentences.

This activity is designed for students to let thoughts flow from their mind to their paper without focusing on conventions, mechanics, or revisions for approximately 5 to 10 minutes. Ideally, students ramble on paper generating ideas, words, phrases, and possibly a brief doodle, developing writing fluency (See **DOODLES-TO-DETAILS**). Initially, you may have to provide a "prompt" and model the process many times over. This prompt might be a picture of a family at the beach, a bouquet of flowers on a table, or a topic on which to write. A teacher-selected topic could focus on a student's background knowledge in connection with current events, literature, or a content area of study.

As students become more and more familiar with the process of "I Don't Know What To Write" they will begin to self-select topics on which they have an interest. Someone may write about their evening at the movies, another their favorite Saturday morning cartoon, and yet another on a problem they are having with their best friend. Because students write for a variety of purposes, their minds may jump from topic to topic as they write. This will develop the critical element of writing fluency. What if, for some reason, a student cannot think of anything to write? Well, they write: "I Don't Know What To Write" until something comes to their mind. It will not take long before they are off and writing! Those are our expectations!

A timer can be used to signal the end of a session. At the conclusion of the "I Don't Know What To Write" session it is extremely important that students be allowed to share. It is always interesting to hear the moans, sighs, and groans of those who want to continue writing. You will actually here, "Do we have to stop?"

This type of unfocused, unstructured, and informal writing will lead your students to topics that they will want to publish. Even if their writing is never developed into a "polished" final product, students are learning to collect and explore ideas, all-the-while, learning a strategy to assist them in getting a piece of writing started.

PIGGYBACKING

Starting a story without knowing where you are going or where to begin can be a little scary. Yet many successful writers' best stories have started with only one or two sentences. Piggybacking is really "process writing" coming full circle, and it will include many of the strategies included throughout this book. From brainstorming, drafting, editing, and revising will come a published piece of student writing. That is the essence of Piggybacking.

When children participate in "I Don't Know What To Write," they are filled with a lot of energy towards writing. Often the hardest part about writing anything is simply getting started. That is where Piggybacking comes into play. After students have had a chance at approximately two weeks of "I Don't Know What To Write" entries, it is time for them to select one of those topics for further development, or come up with one of their own.

So, we have designed Piggybacking as a means of retrieving ideas from a student's Writer's Journal, or asking other students for possible ideas that they have logged in their journals. Students should identify and develop topics important to their own liking! Let them consider several ideas before settling on the topic of their choosing. Yes, throughout this entire process you may have a student change their mind, sometimes more than once!

Why make a student finish a solander? A solander is any topic that seems promising at first, but turns out to be hollow, empty, and barren. It is hollow, as much a trick, as those boxes which people make by cutting out the center of a book and gluing together the edges of the pages to conceal something. There are many reasons for this to occur. The writer may lose interest, have little knowledge, or just not care about the topic altogether. The writer must have something to say! So let them change in order for them to be successful.

We do not want students to feel pressure in conceiving a whole story even before putting down the first word. The above reference of a solander does just that. It allows students to take ownership of their own writing process. Would you like to have the opportunity to write about something you were interested in, or change your mind about something you have written?

After modeling the process of selecting a topic with the whole class, consider a collaborative class writing assignment. Walk your students through the entire writing process. You may have to do this a few times before your students feel comfortable trying this on their own. Too frequently we just assign topics. Our students have become reliant upon us for writing ideas. Piggybacking gradually releases responsibility and ownership of process writing to the students. This is where it rightfully belongs.

DOODLES-TO-DETAILS

As the name implies, Doodles-To-Details allows students to have an opportunity to quickly draw what they know about a subject, or sketch what it is they plan on writing about. After drawing or sketching, students begin to label the details of their picture. Labeling of the doodle allows for precise vocabulary and story elements. It is not intended to be a masterpiece that hangs in an art gallery. Note: Doodling **does not** require crayons or markers. This is not an art activity.

For most students, a visual image helps them to expand upon what they already know and demonstrate an understanding of the writing process. Visuals are powerful tools for communicating information. They act as a springboard to powerful vocabulary, heighten discussions, and prepare students for writing.

Students prepare themselves for writing by doodling. This process intensifies their awareness of word choice and helps them organize their thoughts. Pictures provide for characters, setting, problems and solutions, main ideas, and other important elements of writing: beginning, middle, and end.

For students in the primary grades, an oral retelling of their picture with the teacher taking dictation may work best. Intermediate aged children (grades 3-5) will do best with an oral retelling of their doodle before detailing it and writing about their topic (doodle). Middle and high school students would probably love the opportunity to draw before they write! We would be willing to bet they have not drawn in quite some time, and probably have not been allowed to by their teachers.

The Doodles-To-Details strategy helps struggling students, especially when they need to organize their thoughts. You might ask, "Can more than one doodle be drawn?" Yes!

WORD MANIA

The Word Mania strategy is an adaptation of Linda Hoyt's (1999) Alphabox Strategy, from *Revisit, Reflect, Retell: Strategies for Improving Reading Comprehension*. It can be used for vocabulary enhancement, building background knowledge, or as a reading comprehension activity. Students are given a grid with the 26 letters of the alphabet. They should insert their words into the appropriate grid as they come across ideas, vocabulary, or "connections" they have made to the lesson's objective. It is a great activity that generates questions for discussion, and completely engages students in their quest to fill the Word Mania Grid. Of course that is not the goal of the activity!

Word Mania is designed to have students use powerful words, instead of small simplistic words that they so generally use. Many of the boxes could possibly have three or four words, whereas, another letter grid may be blank. Spelling should not be an issue, either! Students are allowed to spell as best they can, for this is not a spelling exam, only a brainstorming activity.

After students have completed this part of the assignment, many other activities can be spawned. For example: clustering words for main ideas, compiling a class Word Mania chart, drawing a picture that compliments the vocabulary, writing a story, or a paragraph.

Sample: A 4th grade class is going to study the Civil War. Before we begin studying, we use the Word Mania Grid to list words we believe might be associated with that topic. As we read and learn about history and the Civil War, we continue to fill out our grids. Here is what it might look like:

A	B	C	D
afraid	blood	Confederate	
	battle	cannon fire	

E	F	G	H
	freedom	General	horses

I	J	K	L
	journey		Lee

M	N	O	P
men	night		

Q	R	S	T
	religion	soldier	travel
	rifles	scared	

U	V	W	XYZ
Union	victory	war	

WORD MANIA GRID

A	B	C
D	E	F
G	H	I
J	K	L
M	N	O
P	Q	R
S	T	U
V	W	XYZ

SENTENCE EXTENSION

Students sometimes write short sentences that have little description or depth. Sentence Extension is an activity that helps students turn short, choppy sentences into longer, vivid sentences. The objective of this activity is for students to learn how to paint mental pictures with their writing, thereby creating quality writing and capturing the reader of their work. By practicing Sentence Extension, students will naturally begin to do this to their own piece of writing.

You will need a Sentence Supply container that will have twenty to thirty short, very basic sentences where students can pick a sentence.

DIRECTIONS:

1.   Students will find one of the prepared sentences from the **"SENTENCE SUPPLY"** container and write it down.

2.   They will then choose their first **sentence extension** word (who, what, when, where, why, or how) and write it on the blank. _____. Now they will extend their sentence from step #1.

3.   After rewriting the sentence they wrote in step #2, they will select a different **sentence extension** word and write it on the blank. _____. Now they will extend the sentence again.

4.   They will rewrite the sentence they wrote in step #3 and pick one more **sentence extension** word and write it on the blank. _____. They will extend the sentence again.

❖ Students should check over their completed sentence from step #4 for spelling and capitalization and make any needed corrections.

ENRICHMENT:

Use the completed sentence from step #4. See how many different ways students can rearrange it to convey the same message. They may also use the backside of this paper for additional practice space.

SENTENCE COMBINING

Sentence Combining was developed by Herb Hrebic in his writing program titled *Stack the Deck*. Sentence Combining will sensitize students to methods by which ideas are expressed and related in their reading material, and will help them to develop their ability to compose and comprehend. In essence, it effectively stresses the importance of the reading and writing connection. Your sentence combining instruction will require students to synthesize two or three small sentences into one longer, more complex sentence. Attention should be placed upon "how sentences sound" rather than any set rule.

At the heart of teaching Sentence Combining are the four sentence manipulatory skills: Combining, Rearranging, Subtracting, and Expanding. The mastery of these skills will improve your students' syntactic fluency as well as provide them with a writer's vocabulary that will assist them in the revision process.

COMBINE: (ADD)
  ❖ Can they change the opening sentence and provide a better lead?
  ❖ To make the sentences more interesting, they need to combine them for the reader.
REARRANGE: (MOVE)
  ❖ Can they change the order of the sentences to avoid repeating dull beginnings?
  ❖ Key ideas should be placed strategically in a position of importance.
SUBTRACT: (TAKE AWAY)
  ❖ Take out the unneeded words that just fill up space. (Words that lack specificity)
  ❖ Are they focused or off topic?
EXPAND: (STRETCH)
  ❖ Students should ask themselves: who, what, when, where, why, and how type questions.
  ❖ If they omitted information, go back and expand where it is needed.

Use this example below, or one similar for classroom modeling. Write the four sentences on the board or overhead projector.

There is a dog. The dog is big. There is an ocean. The dog swam.

Ask for a volunteer to orally make one sentence out of these four, as quickly as possible. A response might be something like this:

The big dog swam in the ocean. **(OR)** There is a big dog that swam in the ocean.

The students just accomplished the following:

  ❖ They **combined** the four sentences into one.
  ❖ They **rearranged** words, putting big before dog.
  ❖ They **subtracted** unnecessary words. (is, over and over)
  ❖ They **expanded**, adding <u>the</u> or <u>in</u>.

This oral skill will transfer into a writing skill, which is the objective of this activity.

TRAFFIC COURT

For a fun and creative way to manage your students' conventions, try Traffic Court, using different colored markers for proofreading. This strategy, like all the others, should be modeled several times before letting students do this in a center or writing workshop. The objective of this activity is not only for students to learn how to edit their own writing but to realize that writers take many looks at their drafts before making it public.

- ❖ **Green stands for capitalizing beginnings of sentences and proper nouns.**
- ❖ **Red stands for ending punctuation.**
- ❖ **Yellow stands for spelling errors.**
- ❖ **Blue stands for replacing "plain" words with precise language.**
- ❖ **Black stands for other punctuation marks and insertions.**

1. Begin by asking a student, privately, to volunteer their paper for this activity. You should make sure that the name is covered.

2. Using a **green** marker, trace over the first letter of the beginning word of the sentence. Now look for the stopping point of the sentence (hence **red**). Repeat this process throughout this piece of writing alternating from **green** to **red**. After this is completed, reread the piece of writing out loud.

3. Read the piece of writing again, and use the **yellow** marker to highlight the words that could be misspelled (and will check later).

4. Using the **blue** marker, reread the writing and circle the boring words and replace them with powerful words.

5. Finally, use the **black** marker while rereading the writing looking to insert words, quotation marks, and commas.

6. After modeling this procedure several times, students should be able to exchange papers with another student and repeat the process, working together on one piece of writing at a time.

7. Each time students proofread a paper; they should only be looking for one particular type of correction at a time.

First grade children should be mastering green and red. Second grade students should review green and red, and then be introduced to yellow. Third grade students should begin the year reviewing green, red, and yellow, and then be introduced to blue. As the year comes to a close, they could be introduced to black. Fourth grade students should begin by reviewing green, red, yellow, and blue, then, instruction can begin with black. For students in fifth grade, green, red, yellow, blue, and black can be reviewed.

Middle and high school students should emphasize the use of precise language while continuing to be aware of the proper use of conventions.

ADDING SPICE TO WRITING

There are many poetic devices that help to enhance a writing piece. Adding figurative language to writing not only grabs the reader but also helps to form a mental picture of what the writer is trying to convey. Reading literature, poetry, short stories, and even song lyrics help to expose your students to ways that authors use this technique in their writing.

ONOMATOPOEIA

Onomatopoeia is a writing device in which writers use sound words to make their writing come alive and more interesting. Sound words are just every day noises that objects, animals, and even people make sometimes on their own and sometimes with a little help. These sounds go unnoticed until you train your ears to hear them. We all know the annoying sound that a fly makes when it is *buzzing* around our ears. A little mouse can be heard *squeaking* around a piece of cheese. Leaves *rustle* as the autumn wind comes upon a pile of leaves waiting to be raked up. A great place to find examples of onomatopoeia is the comics! Here are a few more:

bark	plop
chirp	screech
fizz	splash
hiss	zoom

WORD PAIRS

Word pairs are pairs of words that have some type of connection. Through constant use, they have become part of our everyday language and are usually spoken together whenever used. When put into sentences, these word pairs have further meanings than when just standing alone. Here are a few examples:

rock & roll	Let's rock and roll.
meat & potatoes	I'm a meat and potatoes man.
sugar & spice	She's sugar and spice and everything nice.
hustle & bustle	It's a hustle and bustle world out there.

TRIADS

Triads are just like word pairs but are grouped in threes.

Hip, Hip, Hooray
Red, White & Blue
Lion, Scarecrow & Tinman
Student, Teacher, & Parent
Good, Bad & Ugly
Snap, Crackle, & Pop

SHARING THE PEN

The objective of this activity is for students to collectively write a story without talking to each other about its content. Yes, it is designed to be an activity that does not allow for any talking between players. As such, it will require students to read for contextual clues as they are waiting for their next turn.

Prepare for the activity by clearing the chalkboard or posting chart paper on an easel. Explain the process to your students.

The first player probably has the most important position, starting the writing off with a powerful first word for the very first sentence. *(We do not let our students start with: One, Once, or I.)* Select a student to come forward and begin the writing process. Give them the pen, and ask them to write the first word, legibly, so others can read their writing.

This student then hands the marker off to the next student. This new player then writes the next word to the sentence, and so on. *(Do not tell your students that they are developing a topic sentence.)*

As this process continues, punctuation will need to be added. Here is the rule:

When it is another student's turn, they must add a new word where the last student left off. If after they add their word, a sentence ends, they should put in the appropriate ending punctuation mark.

As soon as the first sentence has been completed (topic), students will continue to add details until the activity is completed. *(Students are developing details to support their topic.)*

Oops! What if someone misspells or omits a word? During their turn with the pen, they add a new word where the previous student left off. However, they may also make any needed spelling corrections, and insertions where necessary.

Class members can even be divided up into teams, so each student will have more opportunities to pen. The first team, whose players complete the assignment, with all words spelled correctly, will be the winner! However, if a sentence, or sentences are incomplete, the rotation of turns must continue until the story is finished.

ABC ALLITERATION

This is a combination oral and written activity for students to use and manipulate words in expressive fashions. Play this simply for enjoyment and your students will have a blast.

One of the best things about this activity is that it requires absolutely no materials, unless you would like your students to write responses.

Begin by explaining the process students will go through. You might even ask if they know anything about alliteration. Give your students a few examples, making it easier for primary aged students. Middle and high school students should be able to really come up with some creative lines! Watch out!

The object of the game is to go through the entire alphabet, each player using as many words as possible with a particular letter. Before you begin, however, we would eliminate the letters Q and X for fairness sake.

We let our students share their ideas orally with a partner (sort of helps to relieve some of the silliness) before having them write their responses.

We will give you an example for the letter "C."

Crazy Christensen can't cross Cousin Carol 'cause her Cookoo for Coco Puffs come in cinnamon crunch flavor.

Note: Not all of the words will begin with the letter that has been assigned. However, the student's role is to begin as many words as they can with their assigned letter. Have fun!

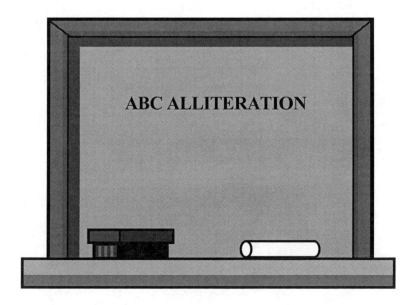

YOU'RE WRONG, I'M RIGHT!

Everyone will enjoy yelling, "You're wrong, I'm right!" to the person trying to change a sentence one word at a time. In this oral activity, (listening skills) students will change one word to clarify the sentence, or make it more ridiculous in an authoritative way.

Students work through this activity better if they are seated in a circle or desks are arranged so students know whose turn it will be next. This is a pass around sentence that will start with the teacher. **(Note: When your students have difficulty remembering, write the sentences on the chalkboard, or overhead as they respond.)**

The teacher begins by saying: " My bicycle has a flat tire."

The next person responds by shouting, "You're wrong, I'm right!" Then proceeds to change one word. Their response: "My bicycle has a square tire."

The next individual begins by shouting, "You're wrong, I'm right!" and alters the sentence by replying: "My train has a square tire." And so on.

The play continues until the last person has had a turn. Allow only a few seconds to pass between players. That is why listening is so important! If someone gets stuck, go on to the next person. Remember, it does not need to make sense.

LIAR, LIAR

Who is the best storyteller in your classroom? This game should turn up the fun while your students invent the most believable, or should we say unbelievable stories they have ever told.

Using some small object (key, watch, shoelace, etc.), students will come up with an incredible story of fantasy to tell the rest of the group. It will be vitally important that this activity be modeled first by you.

Ask for a small object from a student. Let us say that a student gives you pencil shavings. As teachers, we would begin to tell a story, something like this:

> "While deep in the heart of Africa, on a lion expedition, our safari guide
> happened to stumble across an old totem pole. A nearby sign, which
> looked recently posted said: BEWARE! Well, I took out my trusty
> scout knife and carved my initials into the sign. Here, what looks like
> pencil shavings, is really the wood from where I etched my initials into
> the sign. Etc…"

If after you are done the students do not believe the story that you just told them, they yell, "Liar, liar!"

After everyone has had a turn, ask which story your students preferred the best. This person may have the dubious honor of being the least-trusted person in your class.

This activity would probably lend itself better to small cooperative groups. Many of your students could take these ideas, record them into their journals, and use for a further **Piggybacking** topic.

Bill's co-workers began to suspect that he
had lied about having a master's degree
in computer science.

THE BUCK STOPS HERE!

This game requires you to have a small beanbag, rubber ball, or any similar object for students to toss around.

Everyone should stand in a circle. You will begin to tell a story, any story, and make it quick. Do not hold the "buck" for more than 15 seconds. Toss the "buck" to someone in the circle. This person **must** catch the "buck" or the story stops and they yell, "The Buck Stops Here!"

A number of things will happen during a student's turn depending on whether or not they caught the buck.

If they catch the buck:

1. They continue the story.
2. Pass the buck to another person in the circle.
3. Sit down in place, in order for all students to have a turn.

If they drop the buck:

1. They yell, "The Buck Stops Here!"
2. All students stand up again to start over.
3. This student begins by starting a new story and passing the buck.
4. Sit down in place, in order for all students to have a turn.

The object is to pass the "buck" around the circle, without dropping it, and tell a story in the process. The story can take on any form just as long as there is an attempt to connect it to the last player's contribution.

GOOD VS BAD

Each and everyone of our students likes to ham it up every now and then, so we have come up with an activity that will allow you to do this in the confines of the classroom. Students may piggyback off this activity into a writing assignment. It has them comparing and contrasting the good and bad qualities of something.

Ask the students to brainstorm (think) about a favorite person, place, or thing. Next, have them list these qualities on a sheet of blank writing paper (nothing formal, just a piece of paper for jotting ideas). After they have done this, ask them to think of the bad qualities. List them as well.

You might ask them, "What limitations does it have?" Or, "Are there things it cannot do?"

Have each student describe their favorite thing using only its bad qualities. See if the other students can guess what the "something" is.

If the students cannot guess the good thing that they are giving bad clues to, then the students should selectively give their classmates a good clue to aid them in their guess.

The person who guesses what the item or something is gets the next chance to describe something.

For a strange variation, the game may be played in reverse by describing good parts about something bad.

For example: It is not something you store in a house. You do not stand in one of these. Be careful or it will tip over. In the winter, up north, you would not use one, etc...

WRITING SURGERY

Like a doctor who needs precision tools to perform an operation, so do our students when revision time nears. Just how would a doctor be able to perform delicate tasks like setting a broken bone, or surgically repairing a patient's injured heart without bandages or scalpels? Starting the writing process and not having the necessary tools to finish would be similar to the doctor who could not finish operating on a patient because they did not have the staff, equipment, or materials at their disposal.

Students are usually aware that their writing needs work, and they want to add details to certain parts of their writing, but often do not or will not. Many times we have heard very reluctant writers say these words in quite an authoritative manner, "I'm done!" What our students are really telling us is that they do not understand how revision helps their writing. Remember, skills need to become strategies owned by our students. How can we help to accommodate their needs and make this process easier for them?

Cutting and Pasting is a creative way to incorporate new information into their existing drafts. Simply put, students just cut their story up! Yes, they cut their writing apart and tape or glue it onto another piece of paper leaving room for the new extension and elaboration. This process saves a lot of time, and students will be more inclined to add details once they learn they do not have to rewrite their writing in order to insert more information.

We need to do everything we can to make revising fun while encouraging students to play with their revisions. For an additional take on this activity, see if a local doctor's office or hospital would donate surgical clothes to display at the **Editor's Spot**. You might even consider wearing a stethoscope and a doctor's white overcoat when this strategy is introduced.

THE EDITOR'S SPOT

The Editor's Spot is an area of the classroom that has been designated as such. Real writers have certain spots where it all comes together. This happens because they have all the necessary tools in one location. This spot is away from the students' desks.

Once a student has a rough draft, they go over to the Editor's Spot. The student softly reads the draft out loud for possible errors, becoming the first audience.

The Editor's Spot has various editing tools easily accessible for the writer.

❖ A box of colored markers for editing. (See **TRAFFIC COURT**.)

❖ A dictionary and thesaurus for checking word accuracy, spelling, and word choice.

❖ An electronic dictionary could also be appropriate for the center.

❖ A high frequency **Word Wall** list.

❖ Extra paper (lined and unlined), pencils, and even a pen or two.

The Editor's Spot will prove to be an incentive for future writers because they know they can only go there once they have a draft or are ready to publish. For the writers, it is a place of honor because they have made it to the drafting or publishing stage.

It is important for the writers to realize that once they get to the Editor's Spot, their role changes. They go from writer to editor-in-chief of their own writing. They should look at their writing as if it were not their own. This process will allow them to see beyond what is written and what should be written. It will enable them to make revisions without becoming so emotionally involved in the writing.

Listed below are the basic symbols we expect all students to use in the editing and revision process:

¶   Begin a new paragraph.

/   Make a capital letter into a lowercase letter.

∧   Used to indicate where an insertion goes.

=   Make a lowercase letter into a capital letter.

⌁   Deletion mark used to take out words, letters, or phrases.

TRANSITION WORDS BOOKMARKS

EMPHASIZE A POINT

in fact, certainly, indeed,

INTRODUCE EXAMPLES

to, such as, illustrate, in particular, that is, like, as, namely, for instance, for example

CONCLUDE

as a result, finally, last, therefore, in summary, in conclusion

SHOW TIME

about, after, at, before, soon, later, as soon as when, yesterday, first, today, next, finally, second, tomorrow, during, third, until, then, meanwhile

DO NOT SHOW A SPECIFIC TIME

after, next, before, soon, always, first, then, again, at the time, last, while, every time, simultaneously, meanwhile, second, finally, during, preceding

SHOW HOW MUCH

best, worst, first, second, mainly, more importantly, less importantly

ADD INFORMATION

again, also, another, and, besides, next, along, for example, finally, as well

CAUSE & EFFECT

because, since, due to, if…then, as a result of, accordingly, so that, therefore, although, for this reason, so

SHOW COMPARISON

likewise, similarly, as, in the same way, than, also, like, either…nor, either…or,

SHOW LOCATION

above, across, against, along, among, around, beneath, off, near, by, in front of, in back of, beside, below, into, over, inside, down, under, throughout

SHOW CONTRAST

unlike, yet, but, instead, however, in contrast, on the other hand, even though

SPATIAL RELATIONSHIP

behind, below, above, up, here, to the right of, over, on top of, around, beneath, through, here, outside, down, there, under, in the center, on the left side, inside

These transition words help to replace the traditional first, second, third, next, then, and finally words. Adding effective transition words to writing helps to make the writing clearer and more precise.

SAID IS DEAD BOOKMARKS

HAPPY

rejoiced, laughed,
sang out, giggled, joked,
gleeful, overjoyed, glad,
cheerful, joyous

SAD

bawled, sobbed,
agonized, cried,
groaned, sniveled,
blubbered, wept,
lamented, mourned,
sorrowful, depressed,
gloomy

TIRED

mumbled, struggled,
emitted, wearied

BEGGING

beseeched, entreated,
begged, appealed to,
implored, pleaded

PAINED

barked, bellowed, cried,
cried out, yelped,
groaned, screamed,
wailed, roared, howled,
grieved, shrieked

BOSSY

demanded, professed,
bossed, insisted,
preached, dictated,
ordered

FRIGHTENED

quaked, shuddered,
stammered, trembled,
quivered

TO ANSWER

responded, answered,
replied, retorted,
acknowledge

UNDERSTANDING

comforted, consoled,
agreed, accepted,
crooned, empathized,
sympathized

ADDITIONAL SAID
WORDS

added,
babbled, complained,
howled,
jeered, protested,
scoffed,
stuttered, whimpered,
advised,
begged, confessed,
interjected,
taunted, allowed,
blurted,
confided, gasped,
interrupted,
reported, teased, yelled,
barked, demanded,
moaned

These words replace students' overuse of the word "said" in writing.

WHY PUBLISH?

Writing is meant to be shared. How else would we know that Dr. Seuss likes to use rhyme, repetition, and nonsense words? How would we know about Anne's Frank's life throughout the Nazi invasion? Publishing is important for everyone and not just the prolific writer that can write story upon story without any prompting. What about the student that can verbally express ideas, thoughts, and stories but when asked to write them down is stuck?

We have discussed many times throughout this book the need for us to recognize our students' learning styles. In order to reach all of our students, we need to have a variety of ways of sharing writing. You may have heard a moan or two when you tell your students that it is time for a book report. We would like to offer some alternative ways of publishing. They not only will reach your struggling writers but will also encourage diversity and creativity among all of your students.

❖ *Sandwich boards* on posters to promote a favorite book or author.

❖ *Picture books* are an all time favorite for primary students to read. The older students will enjoy making picture books of the main ideas in their book.

❖ *Add a chapter* to a book students have just finished reading. Now the students can extend the ending or add a cliffhanger to a book that left them thinking.

❖ *Pen Pal letters* from one fictitious or real person to another. Columbus may write a letter to Queen Isabella telling her how things are going on the voyage.

❖ *Debate* why living in the North during the Civil War would be better than living in the South.

❖ *Living biographies* are great for the actors in the classroom. They can take a person like Abraham Lincoln and make him come to life using period costumes and props.

❖ *Journals or diaries* are always favorites for girls but consider asking boys to keep a journal of their camping trip, skiing vacation, or a trip to the emergency room that took 5 hours.

❖ *Oral interview* of a famous person in history by having students prepare interview questions for George Washington.

❖ *Autobiographical sketches* are for those artistic students in the classroom. Students get to sketch their favorite character in the book and the changes that occur to this character. They follow this up by labeling the sketches with speech bubbles that the character may have thought or said throughout the book.

❖ *Poetry* can be collected by structure: verse, rhyme, format, or even by subject.

- ❖ ***Bookmarks*** that include who, what, where, when, and why about a book.

- ❖ ***Animal stories*** are always liked by the upper elementary students. Students can take an animal that is being studied in science and give it humanistic qualities and write about a day in the life of.

- ❖ ***How-to books*** involve students explaining how to do a certain procedure. Students can explain how to get to their homes from school.

- ❖ ***Travel brochures*** are fun for the visual and artistic student. Students can work together on promoting the setting of a particular book. The design will include places of interest, historical points to visit and things to do for fun.

- ❖ ***Historical newspapers*** can be an ongoing class project throughout a unit of study. Some sections could include, editorial, want ads, employment, local news, and news from abroad. When studying about the Revolutionary War, there could be an editorial section where writers talk about their opinion of England and what is happening to their country as a result.

- ❖ ***Scavenger hunts*** with clues about where to find main points of action, setting change, character conflicts, etc.

- ❖ ***Comic strips*** that depict a particular episode in the story.

- ❖ ***Flip charts*** depicting particular scenes from a story. Students can pass this activity on to another student to write a description on the back of each scene.

- ❖ ***Class story*** is a project that could be started at the beginning of the school year or class. It will entail a lot of note keeping. Once a week, the class discusses the happenings for that week. They are summarized, organized, edited, and kept as a chapter for the class story. At the end of the year, you will have a weekly diary or journal of what transpired in your classroom. A great end of the year gift for many of your students.

Many of these publishing ideas can be done in cooperative groups, partners, or whole class. Students that read the same book can collaborate on two ideas for one book, or they can work together on the same idea. The goal is to allow students to express themselves with their writing in the way they feel most comfortable.

ALTERNATIVES TO BOOK REPORTS

ABC books	add a chapter
advertisements	all about the author
announcements	anthologies
autobiographies	awards
ballots	bibliographies
bingo (authors and books)	book jackets
bumper stickers (character, scene)	campaign speeches
captions	cartoons
certificates	character biographies
charts of figurative language	comic strips
compare & contrast (books, authors)	complaints
coupons	definitions
dialogue	diagrams
directions	display of artifacts
editorials	evaluations
fairy tales	flip charts (settings, characters)
greeting cards	how-to-do-it
imaginary letters to characters	instructions
journals	labels
letters to the editor	lyrics
maps	menus
mobile (characters, settings)	mural of favorite scene
mysteries	newspaper headlines
persuasive letters	poems
placemats (setting)	postcards
posters	questionnaires
recipes	review
scavenger hunt	schedules
scrapbook collection of reviews	scripts
slogans	study guides
telegrams to a character	thank you notes
time line of events	tongue twisters
travel brochures	used book auction

GRAMMAR AND USAGE

We will define these two terms here:

- ❖ Grammar refers to the structure of a language, and it involves the principles of word and sentence formation.

- ❖ Usage refers to using the appropriate word in a sentence. It is the "socially" preferred way of using language, according to a person's dialect.

Up to this point not one strategy or activity has been mentioned about grammar and usage, this was our intention. In our philosophical beliefs about teaching, we feel that the best approach to teaching grammar and usage is to incorporate instruction during the revising and editing stages of the writing process. Research suggests that this is the best approach, and is the most beneficial manner possible. Locating and correcting errors in students' writing during these stages of the writing process are much less threatening, and much more personal. Our goal should be to assist them to make their paper optimally readable, not perfect! We most likely made a few mistakes throughout this book, but our meaning was conveyed.

Assisting students with the written forms of language in conferences as they revise their drafts usually proves successful. As students manipulate sentences and words, they become more cognitive of the structure of sentences. Through the use of **Cloze** activities students can experiment with the functions of words and phrases within sentences and paragraphs. (See **SENTENCE COMBINING & CLOZE**)

Why do our students come to us unprepared to use language correctly? English grammar is modeled and taught intuitively by those individuals who have the greatest impact upon our students learning to speak. Yes, parents and community members model the dialect that students bring into our classrooms. This dialect, whether formal or informal, differs usually to some degree from the written Standard English that students read, write, and hear in school.

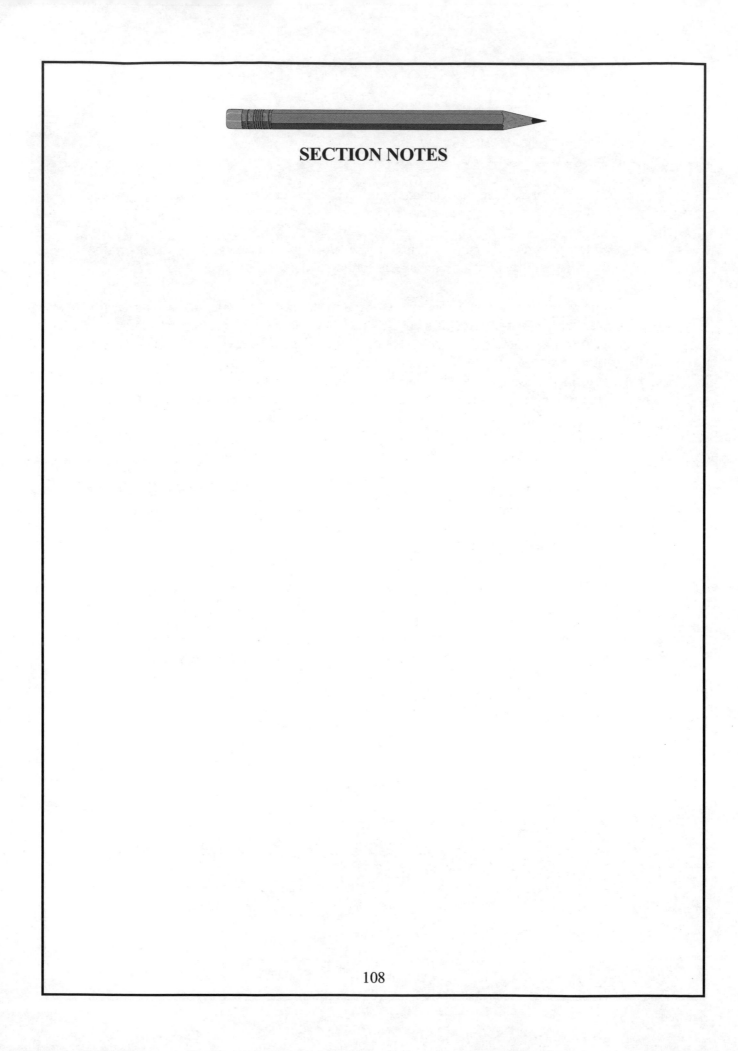

SECTION NOTES

CONCEPT MAP

FLOW CHART

SECTION 5
GRAPHIC ORGANIZERS

VISUAL REPRESENTATIONS

POWER NOTES

STUDENT INTERACTION

GRAPHIC ORGANIZERS

The mind arranges and stores information in an orderly fashion. Graphic organizers are pictorial devices and organizational tools that can be used for reading and writing. These tools help to connect important words and key concepts. The visual quality of the graphic organizer gives a boost to at-risk students. The following are examples of graphic organizers, which your students may use: flow charts, time lines, diagrams, outlines, story planners, feature analysis charts, and semantic or mapping charts.

Using graphic organizers while reading helps the struggling reader understand the structure of the text therefore comprehending the text more clearly. With narrative texts, organizers help to organize beginning, middle and end, plot, setting, characters, theme, or point of view. With expository text, organizers help to explain or tell about a subject, sequence, list, describe, give cause and effect, or identify problem-solution.

Graphic organizers can be used to map out new vocabulary words, organize facts before, during, and after reading or even for sentence building. One specific organizer that enhances vocabulary development is **Word Mania**. It requires students to brainstorm powerful words according to a specific topic and record their findings in the **Word Mania Grid**.

As a prewriting tool, graphic organizers help to keep writing focused and on topic. They also provide a balance of needed information in order to produce quality writing. A visual graphic containing key ideas is easier to remember than just jotting down a list of random disjointed ideas. They also help to form an outline of main ideas, which in turn assist the student to write a brief summary keeping to the key concepts.

Keep in mind that not all students need graphic organizers in order to structure their writing and some formats may be more appropriate for certain types of materials or topics. An over reliance on them can hinder creativity in those students that are born writing creatively. We must remember that not all of our students are in the visual/spatial, or logical/mathematical intelligence category according to Gardner's Multiple Intelligences. Many of our students respond best to the verbal/linguistic, or body/kinesthetic forms of communication. It is important, therefore, to allow for individual differences between our students.

The use of both visual and verbal language to fill out a graphic organizer, results in active listening. This is easily accomplished in cooperative learning groups as participants discuss and analyze visual relationships and key concepts.

The following pages contain numerous graphic organizers, many of which you will be familiar with and accustomed to using. For more information regarding their usage contact us at **www.readingandwritingstrategically.com** and we will answer your questions.

VENN DIAGRAM

Venn diagrams are a great way for students to compare and contrast words. Write the similarities in the overlapping shapes and the differences in the individual shapes.

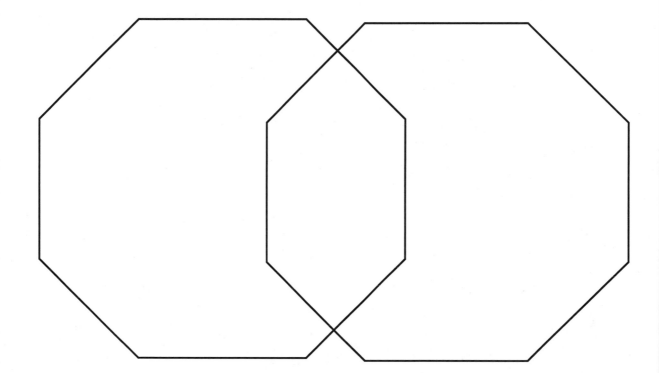

KWL

One of the most effective strategies is Donna Ogle's KWL. It involves three overlapping events: students brainstorm what they already **KNOW** (**K**), record what they **WANT** (**W**) to know, and then list what they have **LEARNED** (**L**) during and/or at the end of the lesson, activity, or unit.

What do you **KNOW**?	What do you **WANT** to know?	What did you **LEARN**?

112

FACTS-QUESTIONS-RESPONSES

Facts-Questions-Responses is an adaptation of Donna Ogle's **KWL**. The strategy involves three overlapping events: students brainstorm what **FACTS** they already know, formulate **QUESTIONS** which they want to find answers to, and then record their **RESPONSES** on what they learned about a new topic of study.

FACTS	QUESTIONS	RESPONSES

STORY READING BOARD

CLIMAX:

AFTER THAT:

SOLUTION:

THEN:

NEXT:

ENDING:

FIRST:

PROBLEM:

CHARACTERS:	WHEN:	SETTING:

STORY MAP

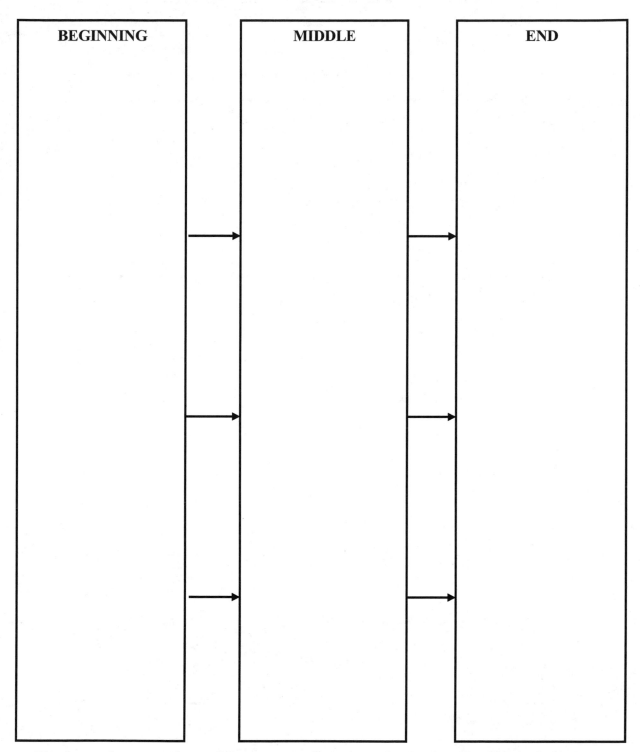

| BEGINNING | MIDDLE | END |

The three columns can be used to compare and contrast many books. Simply sub-divide each section. This format would be particularly handy when studying one author's books.

STORY PLAN

CHARACTER(S)

SETTING

PROBLEM

EVENTS OF STORY

RESOLUTION

END THE CYCLE

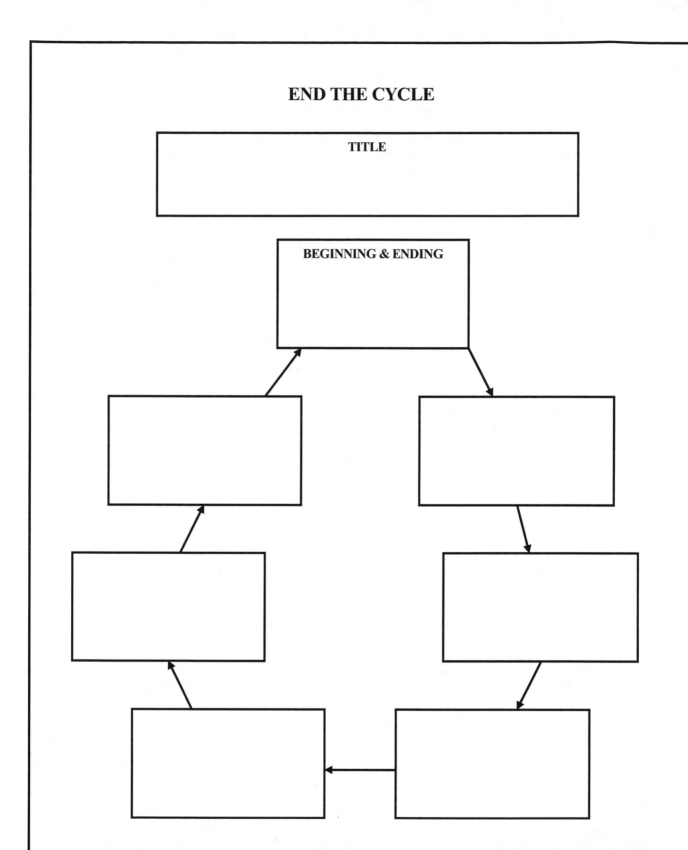

TITLE

BEGINNING & ENDING

Place your title in the top box. Begin writing in the box labeled **BEGINNING & ENDING**. Continue to work in a clockwise fashion following the arrows. Two books that will help to demonstrate this organizer are: *If You Give a Mouse a Cookie* and *If You Give a Moose a Muffin* by Laura Joffe Numeroff.

WORD SORTING

(blank box)

MAIN IDEA	MAIN IDEA	MAIN IDEA	MAIN IDEA

1. _____	1. _____	1. _____	1. _____
2. _____	2. _____	2. _____	2. _____
3. _____	3. _____	3. _____	3. _____
4. _____	4. _____	4. _____	4. _____
5. _____	5. _____	5. _____	5. _____
6. _____	6. _____	6. _____	6. _____
7. _____	7. _____	7. _____	7. _____

The top box is for vocabulary words associated with your unit of study, reading book, or a prewriting cluster of words. The four boxes below are used for main ideas. The numbered lines will be your detail words.

CONCEPT MAP

Place the word or concept you want students to review in the oval in the center of the page. On each of the main lines branching off the oval, write a related category or topic, such as opposites, people, or places. Then, ask students to complete each section by finding words connected to each category.

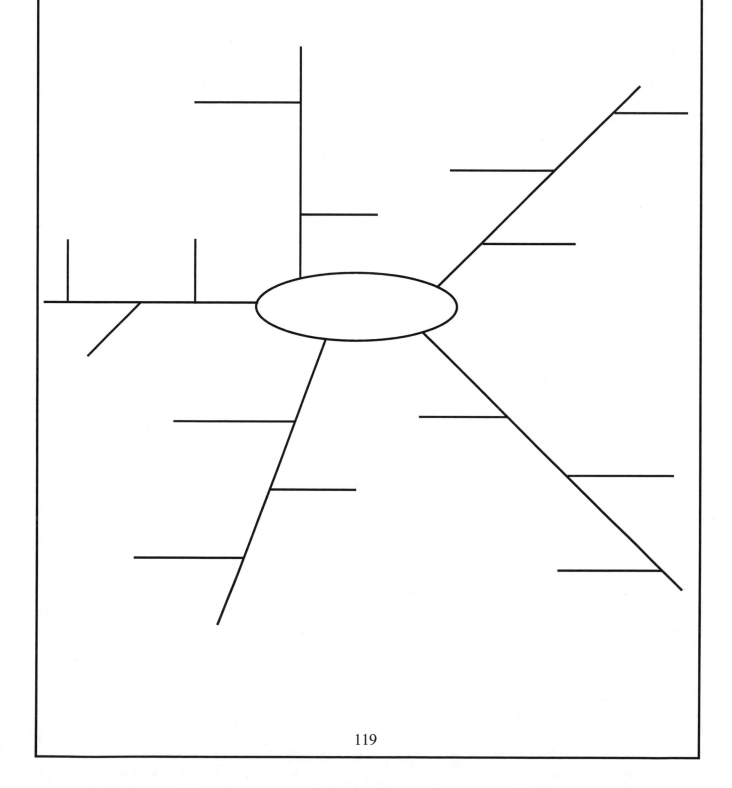

WORD CONNECTION WEB

Select one vocabulary word and brainstorm a list of words related to it. The words can be connected in any way, including synonyms, antonyms, examples, or references to the word in a story. After students have collected a list of words, they should break the list into categories and sort the words into each category.

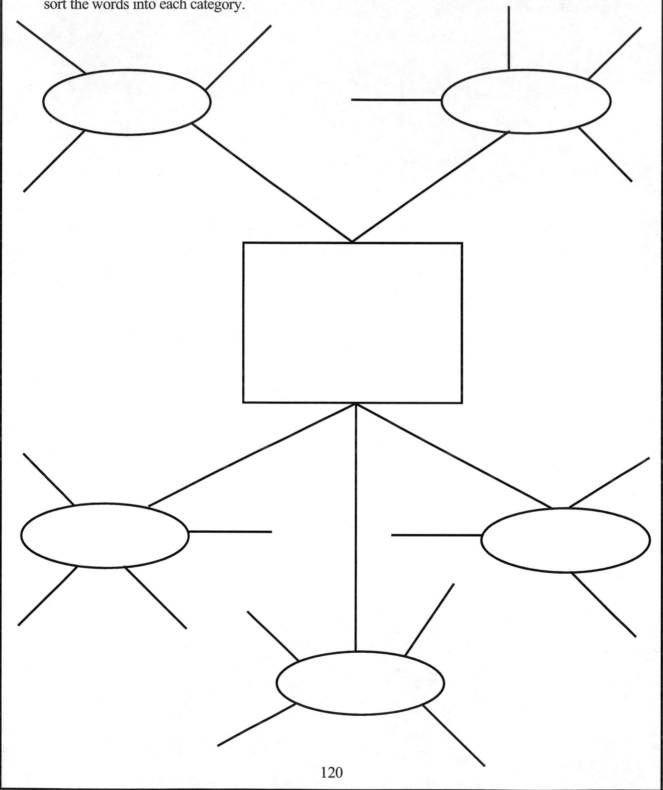

BUILD-A-SENTENCE

WHO? (SUBJECT)	WHAT? (VERB)	WHY? (PREPOSITIONAL PHRASE)	WHEN? (ADVERB)	WHERE? (OBJECT)

This activity is similar to **Sentence Extension** and **Sentence Combining**.

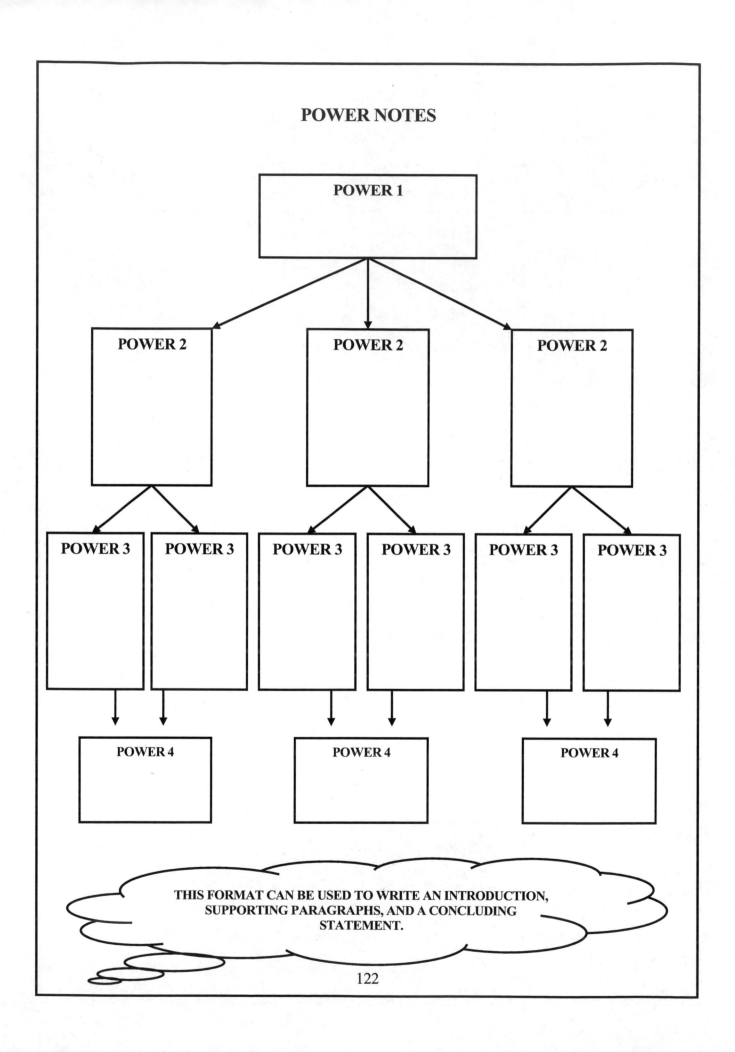

NARRATIVE WRITING

CLIMAX:

AFTER THAT:

SOLUTION:

THEN:

NEXT:

ENDING:

FIRST:

PROBLEM:

CHARACTERS:	WHEN:	SETTING:

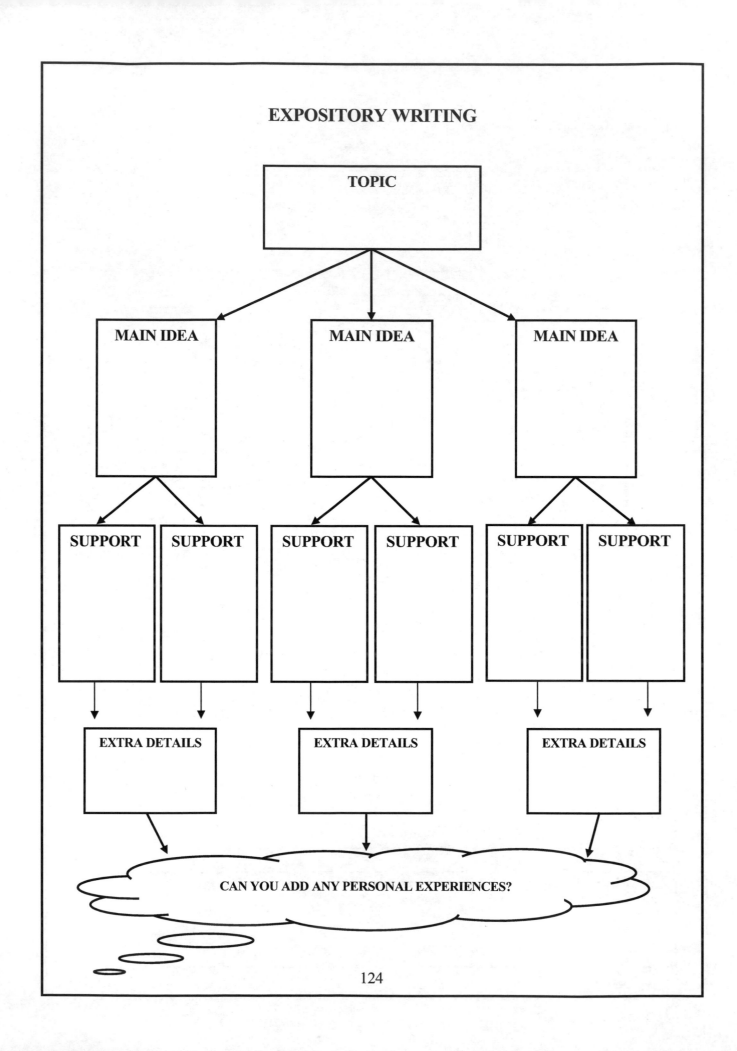

EXPOSITORY WRITING

TOPIC

MAIN IDEA

MAIN IDEA

MAIN IDEA

SUPPORT

SUPPORT

SUPPORT

SUPPORT

SUPPORT

SUPPORT

EXTRA DETAILS

EXTRA DETAILS

EXTRA DETAILS

CAN YOU ADD ANY PERSONAL EXPERIENCES?

NO BRICK WALL IS TOO HIGH

DISCUSS SUCCESS

SECTION 6
REFLECTION AND REFERENCES

ON YOUR MARK, GET SET, GO!

REPERTOIRE OF STRATEGIES

SET GOALS & OBJECTIVES

CLOSING THOUGHTS

Reading and Writing Strategically is a book that we hope you will use as frequently as you can or need to. We hope it will not be put on the shelf with the other books you have purchased throughout the years. Our book is filled with <u>page</u> after <u>page</u> of strategies and activities that can be easily implemented immediately. We have been very selective in their choice, all the while as not to overwhelm you with a lot of fluff and redundancy. They are the best of the best in our eyes, and hopefully yours!

We would like to take this opportunity to review some final but very important thoughts. We can "raise the bar of expectations" not only for our students but for ourselves too. Our students will give us only what is expected of them, so remember to guide, model and assist them to be their best, as we are our best. Additionally, when students are given time limits, they will adhere to them while they work more efficiently turning their learned skills into their quiver of strategies.

The strategies and activities in *Reading and Writing Strategically* do work! Not only will your students want to engage with them, but the transfer of skills will be evident when you see them talking to each other in different contexts. You have probably also noticed that many of the activities overlap and work together. They were designed that way in order to help you organize your time, curriculum and day.

Our classroom environment should be conducive to learning. Students should want to come to a classroom, practically breaking down the door to get in where their thoughts, ideas, and concerns are validated and respected. Classrooms should have walls that teach our students not littered with posters for an upcoming holiday.

Do not be afraid to "think outside the box," and do what is right for your students no matter what your colleagues may be doing. Be creative, different, and enjoy the thrill of teaching! Throughout our book, we continue to mention "higher-order thinking." The days when we told our students what to think are over. They have the knowledge to tell us what they are thinking. We have just never asked them, "A Penny for Your Thoughts?" We need to talk less and listen more.

Be willing to give up the safety net of "status quo." You are the one who is going to be held accountable for your students' academic growth. Your practices may be called into question, and your judgments challenged. However, when you use the strategies in our book and stay informed about the best teaching practices, you will be ready for the challenge set before you.

Change cannot be imposed upon you. Your desire to change in order to benefit students must come from within. We are here to help you each and every step of the way. We believe in what we have compiled in order to help you and your students become successful in this ever changing and demanding world. Please contact either one of us with your comments at **www.readingandwritingstrategically.com**. This website is our way of keeping in touch with other professionals in the business of educating students.

REFERENCES

Allington, R.L. (1996). *Schools that work: Where all children read & write*. New York: Harper Collins.

Allington, R. L. (1999). *Classrooms that work: They Can All Read & Write*. New York: Addison-Wesley Longman.

Anthony, R.J., Johnson, T.D., Mickelson, N.I., & Preece, A. (1991). *Evaluating Literacy: A Perspective for Change*. New Hampshire: Heinemann.

Bear, D.R. Invernizzi, M., Templeton, S. & Johnston, F. (2000). *Words Their Way: Word Study for phonics, vocabulary, & spelling instruction*. Ohio: Merrill.

Blokker, B. (2000). *Professional Development Institute*. Washington.

Buss, K. & Karnowski, L. (2000). *Reading and Writing Literary Genres*. Delaware: IRA

Calkins, L. (1994). *The Art of Teaching Writing*. New Hampshire: Heinemann.

Cunningham, P.M. & Hall, D. P. (1995). *Phonics They Use: Words for reading and writing*. New York: Harper Collins.

Cunningham, P.M. & Hall, D. P. (1997). *Making More Big Words*. California: Good Apple.

Cunningham, P.M. & Hall, D. P. (1998). *Month by Month Phonics for the Upper Grades*. North Carolina: Carson-Dellosa.

Fletcher, R. (1993). *What A Writer Needs*. New Hampshire: Heinemann.

Gambrell, L. B. & Almasi, J.F. (1996) *Lively Discussions! Fostering Engaged Reading* Delaware: IRA.

Gardner, H. (1985). *Frames of Mind: The Theory of Multiple Intelligences*. New York: Basic Books.

Gregson, B. (1982). *The Incredible Indoor Games Book*. California: David S. Lake Publishers.

Graves, D.H. (1983). *Writing: Teachers and Children At Work*. New Hampshire: Heinemann.

Harvey, S. & Goudvis A. (2000). *Strategies That Work: Teaching Comprehension to Enhance Understanding*. Maine: Stenhouse.

Hansen, J. (1987). *When Writers Read*. New Hampshire: Heinemann.

Hoyt, L. (1999). *Revisit, Reflect, Retell: Strategies for Improving Reading Comprehension*. New Hampshire: Heinemann.

Johns, J.L. & Lenski, S.D. (1994). *Improving Reading: A Handbook of Strategies*. Iowa: Kendall Hunt.

Larson-Blair, S.E. & Williams, K.A. (1999). *The Balanced Reading Program: Helping All Students Achieve Success*. Delaware: IRA.

Pavelka, P. (1995). *Making the Connection: Learning Skills Through Literature (K-2)*. New Hampshire: Crystal Springs Books.

Palincscar, A.S. & Brown, A.L. (1984). *Reciprocal teaching of comprehension: fostering & comprehension-monitoring activities*. Cognitive Instruction, 2, 117-175.

Raphael, T.E. (1984). *Teaching Learners about sources of information for answering questions*. Journal of Reading, 27, 303-311.

Readance, J.E., Bean, T.W. & Baldwin, R.S. (1985). *Content Area Literacy: An Integrated Approach*. Iowa: Kendall Hunt.

Robb, L. (1996). *Reading Strategies That Work: Teaching Your Students to Become Better Readers*. New York: Scholastic.

Robb, L. (2000). *Redefining Staff Development: A Collaborative Model for Teachers and Administrators.* New Hampshire: Heinemann.

Santa, C.M., Haven, L.T., & Maycumber, E.M. (1988). *Project CRISS: Creating Independence through Student-owned Strategies.* Iowa: Kendall/Hunt.

Simmons, C. (1996). *Public Speaking Made Simple.* New York: Doubleday.

Steinberg, R. J. & Spear-Swerling, L. (1996). *Off Track: When Poor Readers Become "Learning Disabled."* Colorado: Westview Press.

Tompkins, G.E. (1994). *Teaching Writing: Balancing process & product.* New York: Merrill.

Vaughn, J. L. & Estes, T.H. (1986). *Reading and Reasoning Beyond the Primary Grades.* Boston: Allyn & Bacon, Inc.

Vygotsky, L.S. (1978). *Mind in Society: The development of higher psychological processes.* Massachusetts: Harvard University Press.

Weaver, C. (1998). *Practicing What We Know: Informal Reading Instruction.* Illinois: NCTE

Wong, H.K., & Wong, R. T., (1998). *The First Days of School.* California: Harry K. Wong Publications.

INTERNET SITES

www.readingandwritingstrategically.com
www.stackthedeck.com
www.minipage.com
www.rogerfarr.com
www.ncte.org

For a funny perspective on change in the work place and life, we would like to recommend the following book titled: ***Who Moved My Cheese?*** by Spencer Johnson, M.D. This book will have you looking at your colleagues and others wondering which character of the #1 Bestseller they are most like. It is an A-Mazing tale of Sniff and Scurry (the two mice) and Hem and Haw (the two people) and their search for "Cheese" to feed on and make them happy. Read the book and see which character represents you, when the steady supply of cheese disappears, and CHANGE starts to happen! You may find that at one point or another you are one or a combination of two or more.

STANDARDS FOR THE ENGLISH LANGUAGE ARTS,

by the International Reading Association and the National Council of Teachers of English, Copyright 1996 by the International Reading Association and the National Council of Teachers of English. Reprinted with permission.

The vision guiding these standards is that all students must have the opportunities and resources to develop the language skills they need to pursue life's goals and to participate fully as informed, productive members of society. These standards assume that literacy growth begins before children enter school as they experience and experiment with literacy activities— reading and writing, and associating spoken words with their graphic representations. Recognizing this fact, these standards encourage the development of curriculum and instruction that make productive use of the emerging literacy abilities that children bring to school. Furthermore, the standards provide ample room for the innovation and creativity essential to teaching and learning. They are not prescriptions for particular curriculum or instruction.

Although we represent these standards as a list, we want to emphasize that they are not distinct and separable; they are, in fact, interrelated and should be considered as a whole.

1. Students read a wide range of print and nonprint texts to build an understanding of texts, of themselves, and of the cultures of the United States and the world; to acquire new information; to respond to the needs and demands of society and the workplace; and for personal fulfillment. Among these texts are fiction and nonfiction, classic, and contemporary works.

2. Students read a wide range of literature from many periods in many genres to build an understanding of the many dimensions (e.g., philosophical, ethical, aesthetic) of human experience.

3. Students apply a wide range of strategies to comprehend, interpret, evaluate, and appreciate texts. They draw on their prior experience, their interactions with other readers and writers, their knowledge of word meaning and of other texts, their word identification strategies, and their understanding of textual features (e.g., sound-letter correspondence, sentence structure, context, graphics).

4. Students adjust their use of spoken, written, and visual language (e.g., conventions, style, vocabulary) to communicate effectively with a variety of audiences and for different purposes.

5. Students employ a wide range of strategies as they write and use different writing process elements appropriately to communicate with different audiences for a variety of purposes.

6. Students apply knowledge of language structure, language conventions (e.g., spelling and punctuation), media techniques, figurative language, and genre to create, critique, and discuss print and nonprint texts.

7. Students conduct research on issues and interests by generating ideas and questions, and by posing problems. They gather, evaluate, and synthesize data from a variety of sources (e.g., print and nonprint texts, artifacts, people) to communicate their discoveries in ways that suit their purpose and audience.

8. Students use a variety of technological and informational resources (e.g., libraries, databases, computer networks, video) to gather and synthesize information and to create and communicate knowledge.

9. Students develop an understanding of and respect for diversity in language use, patterns, and dialects across cultures, ethnic groups, geographic regions, and social roles.

10. Students whose first language is not English make use of their first language to develop competency in the English language arts and to develop understanding of content across the curriculum.

11. Students participate as knowledgeable, reflective, creative, and critical members of a variety of literacy communities.

12. Students use spoken, written, and visual language to accomplish their own purposes (e.g., for learning enjoyment, persuasion, and the exchange of information).

NOTES

NOTES

NOTES

NOTES

NOTES

NOTES

NOTES